Quaff 2009

PETER FORRESTAL is a freelance wine writer based in Perth. He is the wine columnist for *STM* (the local *Sunday Times Magazine*) and a regular contributor to *Gourmet Traveller Wine*, the *Qantas Magazine*, and *Money Magazine*. He also collaborates with Oz Clarke on the Australian entries for the *Oz Clarke Pocket Wine Book*. This year saw the closing of *The Bulletin* and the end of a wine-writing gig that he had enjoyed enormously. Being Chairman of Judges for Fine Wine Partners' Australian Wine List of the Year Awards for the first time has been demanding and immensely satisfying. His role as Chairman of Judges for *Gourmet Traveller Wine's* Winemaker of the Year Awards continues to provide him with a fascinating perspective on the Australian wine industry. In spite of its 6 am start time, the Walk with popular beagle, Fling, and impresario Bernie Eastman, is a highlight of each weekday.

Peter was founding editor of *Gourmet Traveller Wine*, and is the author, co-author or editor of 31 books, including *The Global Encyclopedia of Wine*, *Discover Australia: Wineries* and *Margaret River*. In 2008, he judged at the Sydney International Top 100 and the Geographe Show. Peter is a member of the Circle of Wine Writers (UK); FIJEV, the International Federation of Wine & Spirits Journalists & Writers; the Wine Communicators of Australia and the International Slow Food Movement.

Quaff 2009

Peter Forrestal

Hardie Grant Books

Published in 2008
by Hardie Grant Books
85 High Street
Prahran, Victoria 3181, Australia
www.hardiegrant.com.au

ISBN 978 1 74066 671 8

Edited by Clare Coney
Text design by Phil Campbell
Typesetting by Kirby Jones
Printed and bound in Australia by Griffin Press

1 3 5 7 9 10 8 6 4 2

For JJ

John Henry Jens
scourge of the panel chairman, affable wine retailer,
man of many parts, taster, enthusiast, the glue in the social
fabric of the tasting panel ...

and for the light and love of his life, Kate
without whom JJ might well be a high-speed,
blubbering wreck, although still lots of fun.

Contents

Acknowledgements

I thought that no-one but Claire Codrington could stem the deluge of tasting samples which floods the office as yet another edition of *Quaff* comes upon us. That was until Gretchen Dour arrived fresh from a decade in France to break the back of Claire's workload. The work they do is now a breeze: unpacking, cataloguing samples, preparing tastings, that sort of thing.

In spite of their best efforts, her proximity to the action and kind heart means that Elaine Forrestal is called on quite often enough to rein in the (potential) chaos – and, for that, and much more (putting the glasses through the dishwasher, washing the bottle hiders, destaining the tablecloths with Napisan), I am deeply appreciative.

It's been a pretty bleak year for the tasting panel, with Nevile Phillips unbelievably grumpy because of the poor form of the West Coast Eagles. Things did improve from about the halfway point in the season, by which stage Nev had become used to the barrage of losses. Still, he's been a consistently tyrannical and effective chairman and *Quaff* wouldn't happen without his dedication to the cause. JJ, now that he has been elevated to dedicatee, claims to have been meek as a lamb all year (except when Collingwood had a rare win).

I appreciate the camaraderie of Nevile and colleagues Lara Bray, John Jens, Diana Loots, Wendy Roach and Max Veenhuyzens, as well as Rob Bates-Smith and Scott Grieve and a host of others, around the tasting table at 1 Cobb Street.

I acknowledge the support of wine producers and wholesalers who, by supplying samples of their wines, provided the foundation on which the book was built. Our contacts at these wine companies have been unfailingly cooperative and have frequently gone far beyond the call of duty.

In the spirit of the *Quaff* Awards, we announce that Corinna Thompson has won the 2009 'Dot the i's' Award for efficiency. The Reliables: Alex McPherson has been with us for all nine editions of *Quaff* and Margot De Bortoli and Paul Lenon have helped with eight of the nine editions. Last year, I commented that Paul Lenon was handing over the hard work at Westend to Melissa Milani. Well, she disappeared far too quickly and he's slaved away looking after us for another year. Finally, he's had enough and is moving on, so the Reliables will be even thinner on the ground next year. A tribute to one of our favourite people, Hazel Macrae, who has spent the last three years at Liquid Ideas slaving on my behalf (and also Ken Gargett's). Hazel must have had a premonition about the Olympics and has returned to Bleak House, the land of her birth, where she'll become Bunny Macrae once more.

The 'Codrington Medal' this year goes to Corinna Thompson for making Claire's job much easier than it might otherwise be. She has been enormously efficient and a delight to work with. Corinna is the first to win both awards. Awesome!

We would also like to make a fuss over the following for their cheerful hard work on our behalf: Andrew Anderson, Olivia Barrie, Mark Bolton, Paul Boulden, Bly Carpenter, Robyn Clasohm, Scott Darkin, Margot De Bortoli, Charlotte Dowden, Jeannie Duhigg, Hayley Dunn, Gemma Eastwood-Bell, Scott Grieve, Michelle Hall, Louise Harris, Janis Johnston, Bernadette Knight, Paul Lenon, Emmanuel Loucas, Jayne McKennay, Tarsha McShane, Lloyd Meredith, Tiffany Nugan, Eva Pargeter, Kristen Pryce, Matt Redin, Melanie Routledge, Julia Rowse, Natalie Schaefer, Malcolm Stopp, Corinna Thompson, Christina Tulloch, Katherine Ward and Emily White.

I am deeply appreciative of the support, encouragement and quiet calm of those at our publishers, Hardie Grant Books; particularly Jasmin Chua, whose efficiency and gentle manner bring out an author's sense of guilt better than anything. The support of Julie Pinkham and the dazzlingly erudite Clare Coney (and her young border collie Toby and grumpy old kelpie Molly) makes my life as an author much easier. And in Clare's case, makes me appear a much more presentable author. Thanks for the invisible mending. I also love the work of Fran Berry, Jenny Macmillan and Julia Bailey, and acknowledge the contribution that they and the team at Hardie Grant make to the success of the book.

Elaine Forrestal continues to be calm, tolerant, supportive and loving (and increasingly famous – gulp) while the manic extreme youth of the popular beagle, Fling, is a distant memory as he heads for maturity at four.

The bargain hunter's survival guide

An introduction to buying great-value wines

INTRODUCTION

PETER FORRESTAL

In spite of an above-average 2008 harvest, the gradual rise in prices that began in 2007 has continued. The major factor in this has been the continued drought in much of inland Australia and increased costs as a result of the shortage of water. This year, it has been harder to find the kind of bargains we've become used to over the past five years. As prices have risen, in most cases by a couple of dollars, some of our quaffing favourites have a recommended price above $15 but are readily available (on special) for less than $15. The situation is no different from what it's been for several years, except that there is more pressure on the $15 price point.

I expect that with the help of this annual guide and weekly updates on the *Quaff* website you will continue to be able to find plenty of exceptional wines for less than $15. The majority of wines recommended in this book will still comfortably slot into the *Quaff* price point. As in the past, I'll be open and indicate the recommended price. Remember that when this is more than $15, the wine companies have assured us that it will be readily available on special for less than $15. That's why it's in the book.

The strength of the Australian dollar always impacts on the ability of the Australian wine industry to sell overseas and so many of our companies are doing it hard on the export markets at present. This may well mean that they have more wine which they would love to sell domestically. Add to this the surprisingly large and pretty good 2008 vintage, and you might expect that there will be some downward pressure on prices. This might have been the case had it not been for increased costs – mainly associated with the drought and the need for many to pay for water.

There's been pressure on the giant Fosters group, associated with the size of its portfolio and the difficulty its sales force has been having selling from such a vast range of products. Expect some rationalisation there. Constellation has already moved into rationalisation mode, with plans to sell off vineyards in many key regions and wineries such as Goundrey, Leasingham and Stonehaven, and to relocate the Western Australian bottling to Reynell.

The steady march of Coles and Woolworths towards increased domination of the Australian retail world continues. In spite of this, the best of the independent retailers are maintaining a strong presence in the marketplace and both the large chains and the independents are playing a significant part in the increased availability of imported wines in Australia. There's never been such a ready availability of everyday wines from overseas.

It's been a quiet year with *Quaff* online as the promised upgrade has taken longer to realise than expected. We're planning to relaunch the website at the same time as *Quaff 2009* hits the bookshops. As before, it will be a great source of wine information and reviews, and the best way to keep your copy of *Quaff* up to date throughout the year. To receive weekly reviews of great-value wines, subscribe for FREE at **www.quaff.com.au** where we'll let you know as soon as the best new wines under $15 hit the market. Don't forget to tell your friends.

TOP 20 QUAFFING WINES OF 2009

Here is my ranking of the best of the best under $15: the top 'Bloody Goods' (in order) from *Quaff 2009*:

1   2007 Yalumba 'Galway Vintage' Shiraz

2   2006 Kingston Estate Petit Verdot

3   2004 Buller 'Beverford' Durif

4   2008 Westend 'Richland' Sauvignon Blanc

5   2008 Primo Estate 'La Biondina' Colombard Sauvignon Blanc

6   2006 De Bortoli 'Deen Vat 1' Durif

7   2006 Elderton 'E' Shiraz Cabernet

8   2007 Sandalford 'Element' Cabernet Sauvignon

9   2007 Angoves 'Vineyard Select' Chardonnay

10   2008 Thorn Clarke 'Sandpiper' Riesling

11   Banrock Station 'Reserve' Sparkling Shiraz

12   2007 De Bortoli 'Windy Peak' Cabernet Rosé

13   2007 Yalumba 'Y Series' Merlot

14   2005 Bleasdale Malbec

15   2006 Trentham Estate Pinot Noir

16   2008 Kirrihill 'Companions' Riesling Pinot Gris

17   De Bortoli 'Show' Liqueur Muscat

18   2008 Scarpantoni 'Ceres' Rose

19   2007 Queen Adelaide 'Regency Red' Shiraz Cabernet

20   Penfolds 'Club Reserve' Aged Tawny

SOUND THE TRUMPETS ... IT'S THE QUAFF AWARDS

The Quaff 2009 Awards

These are the stand-out wines from the *Quaff* tastings; they represent superlative quality and exceptional value for money.

**THE 2009 OBERON KANT MEMORIAL AWARD FOR THE QUINTESSENTIAL QUAFFER,
THE ULTIMATE AUSTRALIAN WINE UNDER $15 and**
THE QUAFF 2009 'Wagyu Steak and Chips'
RED WINE OF THE YEAR AWARD

2007 Yalumba 'Galway Vintage' Shiraz
One of the high points of the tastings for *Quaff* was the shiraz class. As it happened, the four wines made at Yalumba – 'Galway Vintage' Shiraz, 'Y Series' Shiraz, 'Y Series' Shiraz Viognier and Oxford Landing Shiraz – were next to each other. I wondered what tasting I'd walked into, so brilliant were the four. Best of all was the 'Galway'. This is the 64th vintage that Yalumba has released a 'Galway' red, which for a wine at this price point is remarkable. I've tasted it each year since 2001 (or that's as far back as my database goes) and have liked it each year (except 2004) – and especially so in 2001 and 2002. But in the last couple of years the 'Y Series' Shiraz Viognier and Shiraz have been so good it's been overshadowed. Not so in 2007. It has all the fragrance, depth, texture, structure and balance you'd want in an under-$15 red. It's made by Kevin Glastonbury and sourced from the mighty Barossa. There are plenty of impressive rivals for the title – even at Yalumba – but the 2007 Yalumba 'Galway' is the deserved winner of *Quaff*'s Red Wine of the Year.

THE QUAFF 2009 'Platinum Pillow'
CASK WINE OF THE YEAR AWARD

Hardys 'Reserve' Cabernet Sauvignon
(See page 25.)

THE QUAFF 2009 'You Can Launch My Ship'
SPARKLING WINE OF THE YEAR AWARD

Banrock Station 'Reserve' Sparkling Shiraz
(See page 39.)

THE QUAFF 2009 'Baubles, Bubbles and Beads'
BEST SPARKLING WINE UNDER $10 AWARD

Banrock Station Sparkling Chardonnay Pinot Noir
(See page 34.)

THE QUAFF 2009 'Utterly Delectable'
WHITE WINE OF THE YEAR AWARD

2008 Westend 'Richland' Sauvignon Blanc
(See page 64.)

THE QUAFF 2009 'Light, Bright and Easy'
BEST WHITE WINE UNDER $10 AWARD

2008 De Bortoli 'Sacred Hill' Semillon Sauvignon Blanc
(See page 47.)

THE QUAFF 2009 'Run for the Roses'
PINK WINE OF THE YEAR AWARD

2007 De Bortoli 'Windy Peak' Cabernet Rosé
(See page 91.)

THE QUAFF 2009 'Sausages and Chips'
BEST RED WINE UNDER $10 AWARD

2007 Queen Adelaide 'Regency Red' Shiraz Cabernet
(See page 137.)

THE QUAFF 2009 'Any Port in a Storm'
FORTIFIED WINE OF THE YEAR AWARD

De Bortoli 'Show' Liqueur Muscat
(See page 158.)

THE QUAFF 2009 'A Foreign Affair'
EXOTIC WHITE WINE OF THE YEAR AWARD

2007 Corte Giara Pinot Grigio delle Venezie
(See page 167.)

THE QUAFF 2009 'Another Foreign Affair'
EXOTIC RED WINE OF THE YEAR AWARD

2006 Aradon Rioja
(See page 170.)

THE QUAFF 2009 'For They Are Jolly Good Chaps'
WINERY OF THE YEAR AWARD

Yalumba
This Barossa-based family winery has always been among *Quaff*'s top wineries. This year the performance is unparalleled, with 23 of the 26 Yalumba wines entered being featured in the book. Of the seven 'Y Series' submitted, five were rated 'Bloody Good' and two 'Good'. Once again Yalumba was the top cask producer, with the top three whites and one of the top two reds. Twelve of its 15 casks are recommended and 10 of those are rated at 'Good' or better. The winery won Wine of the Year and was nominated for just about everything. Congratulations to the team from Yalumba.

THE QUAFF 2009 'Move over Darling'
BEST NEW LABEL AWARD

Thorn Clarke 'Sandpiper'
This family-owned Barossa winery is one of the region's largest grapegrowers and it keeps the best for its own wines – as is evident with its success here. Thorn Clarke has excelled with its entry-level Sandpiper range. All six wines were included in *Quaff 2009*, with the Merlot, Red Blend and Riesling achieving 'Bloody Good' ratings, the Shiraz receiving 'Good', while the Cabernet and the bubbly picked up 'Pretty Goods'. It's a label to watch.

THE HALL OF FAME

Stand-out wines

There are two wines that have stood out in every edition of *Quaff* as the best (or close to the best) in their category and have never been rated below 'Bloody Good'. They are not only consistent, but they are consistently brilliant. Of course, I'm speaking of :

Banrock Station 'Reserve' Sparkling Shiraz
Penfolds 'Club Reserve' Aged Tawny

The reliables –
consistent-quality wines, year in, year out

After nine years of sniffing and slurping through thousands of wines for *Quaff*, there are a few that have never failed to impress. The list is slowly reducing in size. However, those which remain have been recommended in every edition, regardless of vintage or label change. *Quaff* salutes the Reliables.

Sparkling

Banrock Station Pinot Noir Chardonnay
Banrock Station Sparkling Shiraz

White

McWilliams 'Hanwood' Chardonnay
Moondah Brook Verdelho
Primo Estate 'La Biondina'
Tahbilk Marsanne
Westend 'Richland' Sauvignon Blanc

Red

Bleasdale Malbec
Peter Lehmann Shiraz Grenache

Sweet and Fortified

Brown Brothers Spatlese Lexia
Penfolds 'Club' Tawny
Penfolds 'Club Reserve' Aged Tawny

HOW THIS BOOK WORKS

We're always looking for good value

Value means tasting – or drinking – a wine, enjoying it immensely, finding out the price and then saying to yourself: **'Crikey, does it really ONLY cost that much?'**

It's being happy to pay more for a wine than you actually paid. It's then – to a certain extent – gaining more enjoyment from that wine because you know you paid a reasonable price for it.

Value is relative, of course. There are plenty of $5 wines that are overpriced, just as there are $50 wines that provide just as much pleasure as wines three or four times the price. This is an important point: good value doesn't necessarily mean cheap. In recognition of this, a whole section of the book has been dedicated to wines over $15 – wines that I reckon offer exceptional value.

But I still believe that **most wine bought in Australia for everyday consumption is still under $15 a bottle**. In fact, about 90% of wine bought in Australia costs less than $15 a bottle. This is certainly where the most dramatic discounting happens. And if you take into account that about 45% of all wines sales are casks, then the average price comes down to significantly less than $15 per 750 ml of wine.

How the wines were chosen

To start with, I approached all the major (and many smaller) wine companies in Australia, and asked them to submit samples of their under-$15 wines for tasting – as long as they would be available commercially from October 2008 until at least the end of the year. Importers were asked to submit wines under $20. I was still receiving and tasting these wines right into August, which means that I was able to evaluate many, many 2008 vintage whites and 2007 reds (even a few 2008 reds) before they hit the retail shelves.

This means that *Quaff* contains more recommendations for wines you can actually go out and buy than any other wine guide.

The wines were all tasted blind – that is, I had no idea of the identity of the wine in the glass in front of me. In my view, this is the only fair way to assess wine: having even the slightest glimpse of the label, or a peek at a distinctive bottle shape, will influence the most determined taster. As always happens, I encountered some surprises: wines with big reputations that tasted very ordinary, and wines that I didn't expect to perform well coming up trumps on the tasting bench.

This year I have included more wines with a recommended retail price above $15 than I usually do. This only occurs when the wineries or distributors insist that the wines will be readily available on special for less than $15 or where I've found this to be the case. When this occurs, I will make the recommended price clear to you.

The list of great-value wines over $15 was compiled from the extensive tastings I do as part of my everyday jobs as a wine writer. Those selected are the best-value offerings of the last 12 months. I have been assured by the wineries that they'll be commercially available at the time of publication and until at least January.

A unique rating system

Some wines are better than others. So, within each chapter on the wines under $15, my selections have been grouped under three headings:

BLOODY GOOD – a delicious example of the style that over delivers on quality and offers great value

GOOD – above-average example of the style that offers good value

PRETTY GOOD – if you're in the local drive-in bottle shop these are the reliable wines you can count on to provide a nice drink.

So while I can recommend about 40% of all the under-$15 wines I tried, I'd only rate about 10% of them 'Bloody Good' – and 60% of the wines tasted I'd happily drive past in that bottle shop rather than drink again (a harsh but fair judgement).

Reading the entries

The reviews are placed within each chapter under the three headings – 'Bloody Good', 'Good' and 'Pretty Good'. In each case, they are in alphabetical order of the wineries from which they come or the brands under which they are sold.

I've tried to make the tasting notes as informative, easy to read and evocative as possible. The often-confusing, technical wine language has been kept to a minimum.

How much is it, and where can I get it?

These are possibly the two most important questions for a wine drinker. And only one of them is easy to answer.

How much is it? When I asked the wine companies to tell us how much their wine cost, they gave me a suggested retail price based on the wholesale price plus tax plus retailer mark-up. But the wine trade in Australia is a dynamic and fluctuating beast, with discounting, local retail patterns and various behind-the-scenes deals and promotions all leading to sometimes quite fluid pricing. So while I can offer the suggested retail price as a guide, you may find that the price on the shelf in your favourite store is different – it will hopefully be lower, but it may be higher.

You will also notice a few wines in the under-$15 chapters with a full suggested retail price of more than $15; we've done this with wines that will be widely and regularly available for less on discount, and made it very clear how much you should be able to find such wines for if you shop around.

Where can you get it? Under-$15 wines tend to be produced in fairly large quantities, so we feel confident in saying that, unless otherwise stipulated, you should be able to find most of them at most bottle shops, fairly easily. Exceptions are self-explanatory: if a wine is only available through one retail chain or direct sales operation, for example, we have indicated that. But to help get you started on the road to discovery – and to finding the less widely available over-$15 wines – we have also included (starting on page 209) contact information for the distributors of all the wines, and listed recommended retailers in each state and territory.

Finally, all wines mentioned (apart from the casks, of course) are 750 ml bottles, unless otherwise specified.

VINTAGE REPORTS: 2008–2003

2008

The 2008 vintage was a surprise packet in so many ways. Firstly, the harvest yielded much greater volumes of fruit than expected, up over 30% on the previous vintage, with a crush of about 1.83 million tonnes. Part of this was due to the break in the drought in many parts of Australia and solid soaking winter rains, as well as a mild and dry period leading to vintage. In much of South Australia and Victoria, the first part of vintage provided near-perfect conditions (McLaren Vale say they were hoping for the best-ever vintage) but this was followed by a prolonged heatwave. Any grapes that were picked before the heatwave made excellent wines but the 15–20% of the crop than remained on the vine shrivelled quickly. The Hunter, Orange and Mudgee suffered from excessive rain during vintage while Western Australia and Tasmania had one of their best-ever seasons. Improved water allocations in the Riverina saw it deliver a record harvest of excellent quality – great news for all lovers of quaffing wines.

2007

For much of Australia, 2007 was a very difficult vintage. Drought, frost, hail, bushfires and poor fruit set in much of Eastern Australia caused drastically reduced yields – down by almost 30% from 1.85 million tonnes in 2006 to 1.34 million tonnes in 2007. While the production of whites fell by 17%, that of red wine was down by nearly 40%. Cool-climate regions, except Tasmania, were decimated, with production dropping by an average of 45%. Unseasonal weather meant that 2007 was one of the earliest vintages on record, two to six weeks ahead of expectation. Fortunately for followers of *Quaff*, good rainfall in January, which helped the vines get through to harvest in better-than-expected condition, meant that the warmer regions of the Riverland and the Murray–Darling did particularly well. The reds could well be exceptional. Other areas to defy the trend and experience very good vintages were the Hunter Valley and Western Australia, where many believe that 2007 could be the best harvest ever.

2006

The 2006 harvest was slightly down on that of the previous year – to 1.85 million tonnes – but would have been higher if some grapes had not been left on the vines because of a surplus in supply. The wine regions in Eastern Australia had one of their earliest vintages following good spring rains, unseasonally warm and dry conditions early in the growing season and cool to warm temperatures from spring to harvest. In many regions, vintage was three weeks ahead of usual, the harvest was compressed and finished significantly earlier than normal. Most winemakers talked about near-perfect conditions and it being an outstanding vintage. The West was less fortunate, with its coolest harvest on record and picking in many places three weeks later than usual. The warmer northern areas did best, producing white wines that looked to have come from significantly cooler regions. White wines performed much better than reds. The vintage was difficult in Margaret River and more problematic further south.

2005

Not only was the 2005 vintage another record one for the Australian wine industry (with 1.92 million tonnes harvested), but it was one of uniformly superb quality. In recent times any increase in the amount harvested has been due to vineyard expansion. In 2005, the increase was due to the ideal weather conditions – a long, mild growing season and perfectly timed rainfall – which resulted in disease-free fruit and higher yields. The exceptions were some parts of the Riverina and eastern Victoria, which were affected by heavy summer rains, and the southern areas of Western Australia, where the late ripening reds suffered because of April rains. Some regions felt that the quality was the best they'd seen in 30 years.

2004

With more than 1.8 million tonnes of grapes harvested, the 2004 vintage was Australia's largest ever – a whopping 25% bigger than 2003's drought-affected crop. There were problems early and late in the season: some of the warmer regions such as the Barossa suffered heat stress (sunburned grapes) in February, and some of the cooler regions such as the Yarra Valley were caught with a few grapes still on the vine when heavy rains hit in April. But between these extremes, quality generally was good to very good. Yields were a little higher than average, too, which eased pressure on the supply of white wines, but only added to the oversupply of reds.

2003

In some ways, a typical Australian vintage – warm and dry – but it was also unusually low-yielding. Indeed, it was the first time for many years that the crop levels were lower than the previous vintage, even with the first harvests from many new vineyards adding to the total. Quality across the board was good to very good, but there were fewer of the superlative wines found in 2002.

Easy drinking at an affordable price

Try the best casks around

TRY THE BEST CASKS AROUND

The media has certainly given good coverage in the past 12 months to one of Australia's greatest environmental issues, the health of the Murray–Darling river system. Of course, this is not just an environmental issue but one that significantly impacts on the ability of the Australian wine industry to make affordable cask wine available. The continuing drought in inland areas affects both the volume of fruit available and its cost. The 2008 vintage, however, has been a significant improvement on the previous harvest. The overall volume was up 31% on 2007, with 1.83 million tonnes crushed (an increase of 430,000 tonnes). Against the general trend in the inland regions, the Riverina delivered a record harvest thanks to more than adequate water allocations. Constellation's Chief Winemaker, Paul Lapsley, commented that its strong increase in production was partly due to the company's ability to purchase temporary water in the Riverland. He noted, 'Some of my highlights this year are Riverland chardonnays with fine lemon flavours, avoiding the broader styles one might expect.'

While quality remains high – a big improvement on the cask wines of five years ago – prices are slowly creeping up. Increased cost of production (especially because of the price of water) is a key factor in this. Still, by world standards, the price of Australia cask wine in relation to its quality is very fair.

The gentle downhill slide in the popularity of cask wines on the Australian market continues. Cask sales continue to represent less than half of the wine sold in Australia – and the amount sold in 2006–07 dropped by 3.2%, down 5.8 million litres to 173.5 million litres. This was almost double the drop of the previous year. In 2007–08, the figure dropped even more dramatically, to just under 160 million litres.

There is about double the amount of cask white sold compared with cask red (white casks are 30.4% of wine sold, reds only 15%). Cask wine remains the most important segment of the market and the everyday choice of most Australian drinkers.

It's hard to believe that this is the ninth year in a row that I've tasted all of the cask wines that I've been able to get access to – about a hundred casks per year. There has been a continuation of the improvements that I noted in the past three editions of *Quaff*, with the best of current red wine casks as good as they've ever been. There is less evidence of chippy oak and dominating added tannins that throw the reds out of balance and leave a powerfully grippy and bitter aftertaste. Of the reds, almost all are labelled varietally, with a few 'dry reds' (fair enough) and only two 'clarets' (they should know better).

The whites too are better than ever. One of the strongest complaints – that cask whites were too sweet – has been addressed. Firstly, well over half of the whites that I received for review were labelled according to the variety or varieties that they contain. There were a few 'soft fruity whites', 'fresh dry whites' (perfectly reasonable) and only one recalcitrant 'moselle soft fruity white'. Consumers will expect traminer riesling to be sweet and chardonnay to be drier. Secondly, wines labelled 'fresh dry white' were generally drier than casks labelled 'soft fruity white' or 'medium white'. There are, of course, heaps of sweet to very sweet cask whites. It's easier to spot them than it was and there is more cask white available that finishes dry or fairly dry.

All the casks listed are non-vintage, unless otherwise specified.

THE QUAFF 2009 'Platinum Pillow'
CASK WINE OF THE YEAR AWARD

On the shortlist for the award are:
Hardys 'Reserve' Cabernet Sauvignon
Yalumba 'Premium Selection' Chardonnay
2007 Yalumba 'Premium Selection' Sauvignon Blanc
2006 Yalumba 'Premium Selection' Shiraz
I loved the Yalumba Sauvignon Blanc, as I have four out of the past five editions of *Quaff*: pure clean fruit, even a tanginess – rare in cask wine. The Yalumba Chardonnay is likewise clean, fresh and varietally correct – a terrific quaffer. The Yalumba Shiraz is probably the best cask red I've seen from the company and a nice counterpoint to the quality it achieves with the variety under the Oxford Landing label, or even better under the Yalumba 'Y Series' label. Last year, there was little to choose between the Hardys Shiraz and its Cabernet, with my vote going to the latter. This year, there was no Shiraz but the **Hardys 'Reserve' Cabernet Sauvignon** was quite superb: great flavour, good depth and length, terrific texture, and a perfectly respectable red. It's the *Quaff* 2009 Cask Wine of the Year.

The reliables – consistent-quality wines, year in, year out

Yalumba, the cask champion of the world, is better than ever. It is unquestionably *Quaff*'s most consistent cask wine producer over each of the nine years that this guide has appeared. This year Yalumba has raised the bar with its performance, having four of the top five cask wines. Twelve of its 15 casks are recommended and 10 of those 12 are rated 'Good' or better. When it comes to casks, if you're not sure buy Yalumba 2 litres. Constellation is impressive, with back-to-back wins with their Hardys Cabernet Sauvignon as the 'Platinum Pillow' recipient and strength across the range (Hardys and Banrock Station are most reliable). De Bortoli underlines its cask credentials by producing an excellent crop of cask reds.

Buying and Drinking Casks – Some Tips

Helpful labelling
On all casks you buy, you'll find a date indicating 'best before' or 'packaged on' (the latter mainly on fortifieds). Obviously, the wine will be freshest when at its youngest – the first three to six months or so after it is packaged. It will tend to get stale at about nine months, although fortifieds may well last longer.

Towards more meaningful names
There have been dramatic changes in all aspects of the cask wine market this year, including the names by which the wines are sold. There continues to be an increase in varietal labelling ('chardonnay', 'shiraz' ...) and this year two-thirds of the casks submitted were labelled with their grape variety. At the same time, there has been an almost complete disappearance of generic labelling ('moselle', 'claret'). While I favour varietal labelling over the use of more generalised names ('fresh dry white', 'soft fruity white'), the latter seem to more accurately suggest their contents than they did a few years ago. At least with the examples recommended here, you can expect 'crisp dry white' to be dry.

The best news of the year, in this respect, has been Yalumba issuing its Reserve Charter which challenges the excessive and indiscriminate use of the term 'reserve' by the Australian wine industry. One result has been the dropping of 'reserve' from the Yalumba casks. I'd love Hardys and De Bortoli to do the same. Furthermore, I'd love to see Yalumba drop the term 'premium selection' from their slightly more expensive cask range.

Let's drop the pretence and call the cask wines what they are: 'Renmano 4-litre Semillon Sauvignon Blanc Chardonnay', 'Yalumba 2-litre Sauvignon Blanc', 'De Bortoli Cabernet Merlot'. These wines are remarkably well-priced and – the best of them – are good quaffing wines that don't need marketing hype.

White Casks

▬ BLOODY GOOD

Yalumba 'Premium Selection' Chardonnay (2 litre) $14.95

This is a first-rate cask white, with fresh, clean, lively fruit that has some richness and concentration – even intensity – of ripe, melony, tropical flavours. Pleasant drinking that represents terrific value.

2007 Yalumba 'Premium Selection' Riesling (2 litre) $14.95

Here is a riesling cask our forebears could only dream of. It's varietal and so made from clean fresh riesling fruit that has some floral aromas and positive lemony flavours. Most importantly, it's pleasantly dry.

2007 Yalumba 'Premium Selection' Sauvignon Blanc (2 litre) $14.95

As honest and as refreshingly flavoursome as the day on which it was first released, this has a lively tang that is rare in cask whites, with pure fruit that finishes clean and zesty. By the narrowest of margins, the pick of the Yalumba whites.

▬ GOOD

Banrock Station Sauvignon Blanc (2 litre) $15.95

There's a floral touch to the aromas of this pleasant sauvignon from Constellation's vineyards at the environmentally friendly Banrock Station: fresh, clean tropical flavours, uncomplicated and easy to drink.

Hardys 'Reserve' Chardonnay (3 litre) $21.95

There's some ripe peachy, melony flavours, a pleasing mouthfeel and soft, easy-drinking fruitiness in this Riverland chardonnay.

2006 Long Flat Chardonnay (1 litre) $9.95
> There's a liveliness to the tiny 1 litre cask that makes the chardonnay appealing: it's fresh, quite intense and deliciously fruity.

Renmano 'Premium' Chardonnay (2 litre) $10.95
> The Riverland fruit delivers smoothly textured, ripe, fruity flavours, and a pleasing soft mouthfeel that puts this wine a cut above many white casks.

Renmano 'Premium Varietal' Semillon Sauvignon Blanc Chardonnay (4 litre) $10.95
> There's some varietal grassiness here, lively fresh flavours and a cleansing dry finish.

2007 Yalumba 'Classic Dry White' (2 litre) $12.95
> There's an abundance of fresh, clean, fruity flavours and a soft, easy-drinking profile that makes it difficult to resist.

2007 Yalumba Colombard Chardonnay (2 litre) $12.95
> This delivers fresh, clean fruity flavours, pleasing texture and a satisfying dry finish that lingers.

2007 Yalumba 'Premium Selection' Semillon Sauvignon Blanc (2 litre) $14.95
> There's some intensity and lively characters here, along with lightly grassy flavours and a clean, refreshing finish. Good drinking.

2007 Yalumba 'Premium Selection' Unwooded Chardonnay (2 litre) $14.95
> There's some intensity and concentration, good viscosity and some generosity before a soft, easy finish. Good flavours, too.

➤ PRETTY GOOD

Banrock Station Chardonnay (2 litre) $15.95

There's some restrained, almost savoury rather than fruity, characters, a pleasing mouthfeel and pleasant easy drinking.

Banrock Station Colombard Chardonnay (1 litre) $10

Pleasant ripe fruity flavours, supple, clean and fresh with a decent dryish finish.

Beelgara sq3 Semillon Sauvignon Blanc (3 litre) $19.95

One of the new range of wine cubes from Riverina producer, Beelgara. I'm not sure that the hype about the packaging is quite justified (stylish 21st-century cubic design is a summer fashion accessory in its own right). However, there are some decent casks in the range. This has some herbal, green grassy flavours before a dry, almost grippy, finish.

Berri 'Fruity Gordo' (5 litre) $15.95

This has positive grapey flavours in abundance, is lively and clean, fleshed out in the mid-palate by sweetness, but has some crispness to finish that balances the sweetness. Will appeal to many.

Coolabah 'Crisp Dry White' (4 litre) $15.95

My pick of the Coolabah whites is clean, fresh and fruity with a pleasing dryish finish that lingers.

De Bortoli 'Premium Reserve' Semillon Sauvignon Blanc
(2 litre) $14.60

There are some clean, lightly grassy flavours here and so this cask is pleasant, easy drinking.

De Bortoli 'Premium' Unwooded Chardonnay (4 litre) $21

> It's easy to drink, restrained as unwooded chardonnay often is, clean, fresh and lively. Good uncomplicated summer drinking.

De Bortoli 'Premium' Verdelho (4 litre) $21

> There are heaps of ripe, sweet tropical fruit flavours here. It's clean and fresh and pretty sweet.

2007 Yalumba 'Premium Selection' Chenin Blanc (2 litre) $14.95

> A decent example of chenin: soft, round and gently sweet with some pleasing fruitiness that will appeal to many.

2007 Yalumba Spatlese Fruity White (2 litre) $12.95

> The exuberant aromatic grapey characters of fruity lexia make it an appealing cask white, especially when its sweetness is restrained (as it is here) and not cloying. Clean and fresh.

Pink Cask

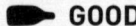 **GOOD**

Beelgara sq3 Rosé (3 litre) $19.95

This is made from Riverina shiraz and is cleaner, fresher and livelier than most. There's quite delicious redcurrant and red berry flavours. While there's plenty of residual sugar to fill out the mid-palate, it finishes crisp and reasonably dry.

Red Casks

▶ BLOODY GOOD

⭐ **Hardys 'Reserve' Cabernet Sauvignon** (3 litre) $21.95
THE QUAFF 2009 'Platinum Pillow'
CASK WINE OF THE YEAR AWARD

As I always do, I allocated the points when I tasted this while not having a clue what the wine was. Then its identity was revealed. I'd given it half a point over its nearest rival. Last year it was the top cask wine and its score makes it *Quaff*'s top red cask once again. I called it a surprise packet last year. I'll be happy to repeat myself. This is the kind of wine that makes casks respectable and which gives the Australian wine industry a good name. It's soft, round and super smooth, almost velvety, has deep, rich and concentrated blackcurrant and dark plum flavours and excellent balanced tannins so its finish is polished, delicate and long.

2006 Yalumba 'Premium Selection' Shiraz (2 litre) $14.95

Here is an outstanding cask red that is very smooth and uncomplicated, with neat balance between ripe fine tannins and deep, rich and concentrated fruit. It's a brilliant example of what makes Yalumba a great cask producer.

▶ GOOD

Banrock Station Shiraz Cabernet (2 litre) $15.95

This is supple, round and plump, and so very inviting, with its ripe dark berry flavours and reasonably balanced tannins. Try with a dish like spaghetti bolognaise.

De Bortoli 'Premium Reserve' Cabernet Merlot (2 litre) $14.60

> I gave these four De Bortoli cask reds the same points so there's not much to split them. This blend of cabernet and merlot has bright, lively, redcurrant flavours and neatly balanced tannins and is drinking very nicely indeed.

De Bortoli 'Premium Reserve' Merlot (2 litre) $14.60

> Looking at the De Bortoli casks in the cold light of day, I'd probably be making a choice between the two varietal ones – so it comes down to whether you prefer merlot or shiraz. This has lively, dark berry, plummy flavours and reasonably balanced tannins. Good with food.

De Bortoli 'Premium Reserve' Shiraz (2 litre) $14.60

> Looking at my notes, I'm thinking that this might be my preferred De Bortoli red cask. It's a touch smoother than the others, with lively, spicy, redcurrant and dark cherry flavours and good balanced tannins.

De Bortoli 'Special Claret' Dry Red (4 litre) $14.50

> I know that some of you will be incredulous about my comments above and will be querying my sanity. If I've given this cask the same points as the other three, and there's twice the volume of wine at pretty much the same price, then this must be the one to buy. My notes indicate that I enjoyed its fruit character although I found it a touch stalky. However, it's clean and fresh and lively, though with reasonably substantial tannins. Perhaps best with a hearty beef or lamb dish.

2007 Long Flat Shiraz (1 litre) $9.95

> This is just what you want in a cask red: soft, round and flavoursome. There's some blackcurrant and dark plum characters and no intrusive tannins so it drinks all too easily.

2006 Yalumba 'Premium Selection' Cabernet Shiraz (2 litre) $14.95
>This is quite bold for a cask red, with a strong oak and tannin influence and powerful, rich and concentrated fruit to match that. Vibrant. A wine to be noticed.

2007 Yalumba 'Premium Selection' Merlot (2 litre) $14.95
>This is a consistently good wine for Yalumba and was rated higher than this last year and the year before. Still, it's a good drink now: clean and fresh with good balance between the tannin slick with which it finishes and its blackberry flavours. Smooth texture. As ever, it's a good food wine – try with roast leg of lamb.

 **PRETTY GOOD**

Banrock Station Cabernet Merlot (2 litre) $15.95
>Has some plump, ripe, plummy flavours, smooth texture and quite firm tannins. Drink with a hearty meat dish.

Beelgara sq3 Cabernet Merlot (3 litre) $19.95
>This has some earthy, blackberry flavours that provide reasonable balance for its substantial tannins. A decent drink.

Coolabah Dry Red (4 litre) $12.50
>This has some attractive red berry flavours and is very easy drinking.

Morris Dry Red (4 litre) $13.50
>While it doesn't have great depth of flavour, it is soft, round and drinks very smoothly.

Renmano 'Premium' Shiraz Cabernet (2 litre) $10.95
>Although this is a bit firmish and has plenty of tannin, there are some honest, earthy dark berry flavours to go with the barbecue sausages.

Fortified Casks

 **GOOD**

De Bortoli Liqueur Muscat (4 litre) $24
>Many will find this hard to resist: sweet raisin, honey and toffee flavours, silky smooth almost lush texture, good richness and concentration before a clean, fresh finish.

McWilliams 'Premium Selection' Tawny Port (2 litre) $11.95
>There are plenty of raisiny characters, a pleasing soft sweetness and a reasonably lush texture before a gentle sweet finish.

Morris Tawny (2 litre) $13.95
>Plenty of raisins here too – big ripe raisiny flavours – and with attractive smooth sweet fruit.

Penfolds Wood Aged Australian Tawny (2 litre) $15.95
>There's a gentle softness, mid-palate sweetness and smooth, raisiny flavours before finishing sweet and pleasant.

Penfolds Wood Aged Muscat (2 litre) $15.95
>This is fresh, clean and pleasantly sweet, with a silky smooth texture and some gentle raisiny characters.

PRETTY GOOD

De Bortoli 'Premium Reserve' Tawny Port (2 litre) $14.60
>Restrained, smooth and pleasant drinking, with some gentle raisiny characters.

More froth than bubble

Sparkling wines under $15

SPARKLING WINES UNDER $15

The sparkling wine market under $15 is as reliably good as it's ever been. In fact, with improvements in technology our bubblies are now cleaner, fresher, less faulty than they've ever been. There are two kinds of cheap sparklers that I would want to avoid: those that are bland and uninteresting and those that have overly strong or powerful acidity. With a guide like *Quaff*, you can avoid them.

In spite of the dramatic rise in the number of rosés on the market, there aren't that many sparkling rosés at our price point. The big increase continues to be in the sweet sparkling wine area, especially with moscatos. At their best, these are just fabulous wines. Most importantly, there are plenty of excellent sparkling wines under $15 still readily available on the Australian market.

Constellation continues to dominate the sparkling wine arena of *Quaff*, with Banrock Station, Sir James, Omni and Leasingham all bringing credit to the multinational company. The Banrock Station Pinot Noir Chardonnay and 'Reserve' Sparkling Shiraz have now been rated 'Bloody Good' in all the nine editions of *Quaff*, with the Pinot Noir Chardonnay winning Best Sparkling Under $10 for the fifth year in a row; and the Banrock Station 'Reserve' Sparkling Shiraz – Wine of the Year in 2005 – winning the Sparkling Red category once more.

Fosters has clearly been putting its sparkling wine effort into the Yellowglen and Wolf Blass ranges: these have been reliably good in recent years and are getting better. Its recent addition to the range – low-alcohol 'Jewel' bubblies – continues to surprise and delight me.

The quality of the De Bortoli 'Emeri' range has soared and it now achieves admirable consistency. Pernod Ricard, too, has delivered good results with Carrington and Orlando 'Trilogy'.

All sparkling wines below are non-vintage, unless otherwise indicated.

THE QUAFF 2009 'You Can Launch My Ship'
SPARKLING WINE OF THE YEAR AWARD

On the shortlist for the award are:
Banrock Station Chardonnay Pinot Noir
Banrock Station 'Reserve' Sparkling Shiraz
De Bortoli 'Emeri' Sparkling Bianco
The quality of the Emeri range has improved significantly in the past few years and De Bortoli is introducing new technology to see that it gets even better. The De Bortoli 'Emeri' Sparkling Bianco is a thirst quencher that is low in alcohol and hard to resist. The **Banrock Station 'Reserve' Sparkling Shiraz** is once again a brilliant example of a quintessential Aussie style – and exactly what *Quaff* is all about, great drinking at a bargain price. It's the *Quaff 2009* Sparkling Wine of the Year.

> **THE QUAFF 2009 'Baubles, Bubbles and Beads'**
> **BEST SPARKLING WINE UNDER $10 AWARD**
>
> On the shortlist for this award are:
> **Banrock Station Chardonnay Pinot Noir**
> **2007 Banrock Station Moscato**
> **2006 Carrington Brut**
> **Carrington Blush**
> The **Banrock Station Chardonnay Pinot Noir** is the best-value bubbly under $10, as it has been for the the the past seven years, and a veritable bargain. It's the only one of the sparkling wines under $10 rated 'Bloody Good' so there's no question about the award. Having said that, the Banrock Station Moscato is a decent, everyday-priced, sweet, low-alcohol semi-sparkling white, the Carrington Blush is a delicious good-quality rosé style and the Carrington Brut is a great party bubbly.

The reliables –
consistent-quality wines, year in, year out

Banrock Station Pinot Noir Chardonnay and Banrock Station 'Reserve' Sparkling Shiraz (2004 Wine of the Year) have appeared in each edition of *Quaff*. The Brown Brothers Moscato (2002 Wine of the Year) has appeared in all but one edition of *Quaff*. The Yellowglen bubblies have been consistent over the past few years and are always a reliable choice.

Buying and Drinking Bubbly – Some Tips

Look for places with a quick turnover
The most impressive wines have clean, fresh, lively, up-front flavours. As these wines don't improve with cellaring, buy from shops that have a quick turnover of stock.

Drink cold
These budget-priced quaffers are best served nicely chilled to enhance their fresh, lively character and zingy acidity. Enjoy and quaff on!

Keep it simple
I've grumbled for a while about the marketing of budget-priced sparkling wines, in particular with the way companies use French words associated with champagne as part of their names. In my view, the use of words like 'brut' (which means 'dry' in French) and 'cuvée' (a blend) are pointless, even silly. What consumer is going to be impressed by the producer adding 'brut', 'brut de brut', 'brut cuvée' or 'grande cuvée' to the name of a bubbly? What will most customers make of the difference between the Sir James 'Cuvée Brut' and the Sir James 'Brut de Brut'? Just as ludicrous is the use of the term 'reserve' to describe these large-volume sparkling wines – especially, as with the Banrock Station Sparkling Shiraz, when there is no standard wine.

Thank goodness for straightforward, no-nonsense marketing and names such as Omni Non-Vintage, Omni Red, Carrington Blush, De Bortoli 'Emeri' Sparkling Sauvignon Blanc, McGuigan 'Black Label' Sparkling Chardonnay Pinot Noir, Brown Brothers 'Zibibbo', Yellowglen 'Yellow' and Banrock Station Pinot Noir Chardonnay.

White Sparkling

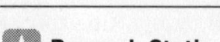 **BLOODY GOOD**

⭐ **Banrock Station Sparkling Chardonnay Pinot Noir** $9

THE QUAFF 2009 'Baubles, Bubbles and Beads'
BEST SPARKLING WINE UNDER $10 AWARD

This is an amazing bubbly. Year after year, it keeps coming up in the *Quaff* tastings as a brilliant-value sparkling wine. For the past seven years, it's been our most consistent budget-priced bubbly. Winemaker Ed Carr is not only a cool guy but, on the evidence of the cheaper Constellation sparkling wines, he is the maestro. You should see the more expensive of his bubblies. Anyway, the current Banrock Station Sparkling Chardonnay Pinot Noir is soft, delicate and fine with attractive yeasty aromas, bright lemon citrus flavours, gentle creamy texture and a gentle dry finish that lingers.

De Bortoli 'Emeri' Sparkling Sauvignon Blanc $13.95

I know. I know. You'd don't expect to see a sparkling sauvignon, much less a sparkling sauvignon with a 'Bloody Good' rating. Well, De Bortoli is just the kind of wine company that can get away with something like this. The bubbly is floral with bright, lively, tropical fruit flavours and some appley characters, very clean and balanced so that some sweetness on the finish is scarcely noticeable. It's very much fruit-driven and delightfully tangy.

Dunes Chardonnay Pinot Noir $14.95

There's a pleasing freshness, lively verging on bold lemony citrus characters with a hint of yeastiness, almost creamy texture, and cleansing, balanced acidity to finish.

Sir James 'Cuvee Brut' Pinot Noir Chardonnay $17

While the price of this two-times *Quaff* Sparkling Wine of the Year winner continues to creep upwards (justifiably, I have to say), it is still available on special for less than $15. When that happens, you won't drink better in the price bracket. The current blend is powerful, bold and intense with yeasty, biscuity aromas, fine, lemony acidity, attractive creamy texture and crisp, dry acidity that refreshes.

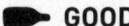 **GOOD**

2006 Carrington Brut $7.95

This is an old favourite from the Pernod Ricard group which is often (as it is now) among the best-value bubblies under $10: it's fresh and vibrant with mid-palate creaminess, and so decent balance, before a finish notable for its powerful cleansing acidity.

Carrington Brut $7.95

There's not much between the current non-vintage and vintage Carringtons, both in terms of style and quality. This has the freshness and vibrancy of the vintage bubbly, similar creamy texture, some yeasty characters, and a dry lingering finish.

Orlando 'Trilogy' Pinot Noir Chardonnay Pinot Meunier $15.95

Another of the Pernod Ricard bubblies, invariably available somewhere in your neighbourhood for less than $15, and a better than average drop. This year it has characteristic freshness, lemon citrus flavours, a pleasant mouthfeel and restrained, cleansing acidity to finish.

Yellowglen 'Jewel' Yellow $13.95

The low-alcohol version of Yellow introduced by Yellowglen last year was a surprisingly (to me anyway) impressive bubbly. The current blend drinks well and many will be attracted to its promise that because of its low alcohol (6%) it has 30% fewer kilojoules than the standard Yellow. Certainly, you can drink more without your sobriety being challenged. There's some lemon citrus perfumes with a hint of yeast, sherberty flavours and a soft, creamy palate.

◗ PRETTY GOOD

Angas Brut $8.95

While I preferred last year's Angas Brut to this, there's still much to attract you to this bubbly. The price, for a start. Moreover, it's clean and fresh with some yeasty characters and pleasing complexity.

Jean Pierre & Co 'Celebration' Brut $7

While I'm not sure about the packaging, the bubbly is sound and attractive and fair value: fresh and clean with some mid-palate creaminess.

Redbank 'Emily' Chardonnay Pinot Noir $13.95

A popular bubbly on cafe lists around the country because it's an easy-drinking style with some intriguing straw characters, a hint of yeast, clean flavours, and balanced acidity.

Sir James 'Brut de Brut' Pinot Noir Chardonnay $17

For an Australian wine company to market two wines with names so similar – one as 'Cuvee Brut' and the other 'Brut de Brut' – is silly. I can't imagine many Australian consumers would pick the subtle distinction that this bubbly is drier than the other. This is clean and well made but I prefer the more interesting other.

Thorn Clarke 'Sandpiper' Pinot Noir Chardonnay $14.95

> A pleasant bubbly from a Barossa label which is not a specialist sparkling wine producer: there's a faint pink tinge, it's fresh and fruity, light-bodied, tight and lean.

Trentham Estate 'Murphy's Lore' Brut Reserve $10

> This will appeal to those who like a gentle, refreshing bubbly with some sweetness.

Wolf Blass 'Red Label' Chardonnay Pinot Noir $13.95

> Here is a nice, easy-drinking sparkling wine with some yeasty characters, delicate soft creamy texture and a fine, gentle finish.

2006 Yellowglen Pinot Noir Chardonnay $16.95

> This is a bubbly that would be terrific with food. In fact, it needs food to tone it down: bold yeasty flavours, creamy texture, and rich, powerful and zesty to finish.

Pink Sparkling

◖ BLOODY GOOD

Omni Pink $12.50

It's that Ed Carr waving his magic wand again and so the current Omni Pink has a soft creamy palate, some ripe strawberry flavours that are clean and fresh, while the finish is balanced and lively.

◖ GOOD

Banrock Station Sparkling White Shiraz $9

This is pretty seductive: ripe, sweet strawberry flavours, soft, easy-drinking, gently creamy, finishing fresh and sweet.

Carrington Blush $7.95

You can't go wrong with Carrington this year. Its rosé style scored similar points to the label's white bubblies. There's just a tinge of light pink, a hint of strawberry aroma; the wine is fresh and lively with pristine fruit, creamy texture and a delightful mouthfeel before a crisp clean finish.

◖ PRETTY GOOD

Yellowglen 'Jewel' Pink $13.95

This has attractive strawberry characters on the nose and palate, some sweetness, and finishes clean and crisp. It is lower in alcohol (and therefore kilojoules) than the Yellowglen Pink and is much softer and less boldly acidic.

Red Sparkling

⬤► **BLOODY GOOD**

⭐ **Banrock Station 'Reserve' Sparkling Shiraz** $13
THE QUAFF 2009 'You Can Launch My Ship'
SPARKLING WINE OF THE YEAR AWARD
This remarkable bubbly continues its run at the top of our
sparkling red division. Along with the Penfolds Reserve
Club Aged Tawny, it has had the longest run at the top of
any wine section in *Quaff*. There was some close competition from within the Constellation portfolio, from a wine
that was rated 'Pretty Good' last year: the 2004 Leasingham
'Magnus' Sparkling Shiraz. A year's bottle age has done
that the world of good. The Banrock Station 'Reserve'
Sparkling Shiraz has the richness and concentration you'd
expect combined with mid-palate softness, almost velvety
texture, vanilla and blackberry flavours.

De Bortoli 'Emeri' Sparkling Shiraz $13.95
There's been huge improvement in the De Bortoli
sparkling wines over the past few years and the 'Emeri'
label now deserves to be rated among the most reliable of
our budget-priced bubblies. Here's more proof: a soft,
round and creamy sparkling red with ripe plummy
flavours and a clean, sweet though balanced finish.

2004 Leasingham 'Magnus' Sparkling Shiraz $16.50
The price is up on what it was a year ago, although that's
the case with most of Australia's budget-priced wines.
However, the year in bottle has done wonders for this Clare
Valley sparkling shiraz. The vanilla bean, oak and ripe plum
jam flavours are still evident and they are pretty bold and in
your face when you first taste the wine. It's softer and more
voluptuous, more seductively creamy in the mid-palate yet
nicely balanced by its weight and power.

▬► GOOD

Omni Red $12.50

>The price rise from under $10 has coincided with a lift in the quality of Omni and so it's fair to say that the wine represents even better value for money than before. Especially as I'm expecting it to be widely available on special for less than ten bucks. This is medium-bodied, has ripe blackberry jam flavours, and an almost syrupy texture that many will love before a cleansing finish that satisfies. A crowd pleaser with good balance.

▬► PRETTY GOOD

Cockatoo Ridge 'Black' Sparkling Red $10

>I was amazed to find two sparkling reds under the Cockatoo Ridge label in the *Quaff* tastings, especially one labelled 'Sparkling Burgundy'. Even apart from the name, this was the one I preferred: with mellow, ripe plummy characters, some depth of flavour, and smooth texture before a lively finish.

Wyndham Estate 'Bin 555' Sparkling Shiraz $14.95

>This is what you'd expect from Wyndham, a traditional sparkling red that is soft, round and easy drinking with good mouthfeel and substantial tannins to finish. Needs food to be at its best: perhaps top-quality barbecue sausages, a sourdough bun and non-commercial tomato sauce.

Yellowglen Red $13.95

>This is softer, rounder, less oaky and less robust than last year's wine, with ripe plummy flavours, still that creamy texture and perceptible sweetness to finish.

Sweet Sparkling

➤ BLOODY GOOD

2008 Brown Brothers Moscato $15.40

It has only missed out once in the nine editions of *Quaff* and this year is back to its best. I found its acidity a little bit too racy last year and the balance is better here. This is fresh and youthful, fine, delicate and deliciously grapey, finishing sweet but with zesty crisp acidity to cleanse the palate.

De Bortoli 'Emeri' Pink Moscato $13.95

I tasted the two 'Emeri' moscatos on different occasions and wrote quite similar notes on how they tasted. As well as its delicate salmon-pink colour, the Pink had delightfully grapey flavours that were full-throttle, sweet on the mid-palate yet finishing clean, fresh and crisp. Still sweet but gently, refreshingly so.

De Bortoli 'Emeri' Sparkling Bianco $13.95

A very attractive moscato style that is fragrant and shows vibrant sweet grape and rose-petal flavours with refreshing crisp acidity to prevent its sweetness from becoming cloying.

2008 Innocent Bystander Moscato $12.50 (375 ml)

Typically of the Innocent Bystander label, the marketing of this is exemplary: clear half bottle with crown seal, gorgeous light pink colour and just enough of this lightly fizzy sweetie to share with someone special. In the blind tasting, too, it was a star: sweet strawberry flavours, fine, delicate and focused, gently sweet before a clean, crisp, lively but gently sweet finish.

2007 Wolf Blass 'Yellow Label' Moscato $17.95

Here is an excellent example of the moscato style: lively and full flavoured with bright, grapey flavours, a fresh zestiness and zingy acidity to relieve the sweetness on the finish. Low in alcohol, too, at 5.5% alcohol by volume.

2008 Yellowglen Bella $17.95

I loved the intense floral aromas, sweet grape, rose-petal, turkish delight and fresh fruit salad flavours (juicy fuji apple, said one of the tasting panel). It's gently sparkling – as you'd expect of moscato and low (7.5%) in alcohol – and finishes with crisp, cleansing acidity.

GOOD

2008 Rosemount Estate O $17.95

There's a lovely fruit purity about this moscato, impressive packaging too. It has gently grapey aromas, is soft and sweet with a lively fresh finish that appears sweeter than most.

PRETTY GOOD

2007 Banrock Station Moscato $9

This is clean, fresh and sweet, with reasonable balance and some crisp liveliness.

Brown Brothers 'Zibibbo' $15.40

This is the second release of a delicious new wine from the Brown family – no doubt sparked off by the success of their Moscato. Like that style of bubbly, it is low in alcohol – at 6% less than half most wines – is sweet, and is made from the muscat grape. The name is the Italian word for muscat. I preferred the crispness of the acidity on last year's debut release of this delicious new style from the Brown Brothers team. However, this is soft and delicate with lovely grapey flavours which linger on the mid-palate and the finish. While most will love the vibrancy and sweet flavours of the wine, I just want a bit more crispness to cleanse that palate and balance the sweetness.

2007 Deakin Estate Moscato $10

This is way too sweet for me but I do like its attractive sweet lime cordial flavours.

2008 Trentham Estate 'La Famiglia' Moscato $14

While I find this too sweet, I realise that there will be plenty of consumers who will love it, and enjoy that Trentham Estate reliability and honest grapey flavour.

Bottled sunshine

White wines under $15

THE QUAFF 2009 'Utterly Delectable'
WHITE WINE OF THE YEAR AWARD

On the shortlist for this award are:
2007 Angoves 'Vineyard Select' Chardonnay
2007 De Bortoli 'Windy Peak' Viognier
2008 Kirrihill 'Companions' Riesling Pinot Gris
2008 Primo Estate 'La Biondina' Colombard Sauvignon Blanc
2008 Thorn Clarke 'Sandpiper' Riesling
2008 Westend 'Richland' Sauvignon Blanc
The Angoves 'Vineyard Select' is a classy chardonnay that is complex and delicious. Primo Estate's little blonde bombshell is great once again – tangy and zesty and so hard to resist – while the well-performed Kirrihill 'Companions' catches me by surprise with a fascinating blend of riesling and pinot gris that works amazingly well. Thorn Clarke has been a model of consistency, too, with the 'Sandpiper' range: this riesling is a beautifully balanced, thrilling white that lingers in the memory. The **2008 Westend 'Richland' Sauvignon Blanc** is as reliable as 'La Biondina' and better than it's ever been – complex, tightly flavoured, and refreshingly taut. It's my White Wine of the Year. Quaff on!

THE QUAFF 2009 'Light, Bright and Easy'
BEST WHITE WINE UNDER $10 AWARD

On the shortlist for this award are:
2008 Angoves 'Long Row' Verdelho
2007 De Bortoli 'Sacred Hill' Semillon Chardonnay
2008 De Bortoli 'Sacred Hill' Semillon Sauvignon Blanc
2008 De Bortoli 'Montage' Semillon Sauvignon Blanc
The Angoves Verdelho is great immediate drinking, fruity, gluggable and satisfying – verdelho that's good enough for a second glass. The team at De Bortoli has had another remarkable year: semillon chardonnay can be bland and dull but not in their hands, and the 2008 'Sacred Hill' has distinct grassy characters and a vibrant finish. I think the SSB is even better – crammed with ripe fruit and with balance and drinkability. The De Bortoli 'Montage' is an excellent quaffer, just a bit less concentrated and a bit less whoosable, if you get my drift. So I'm going for the **2008 De Bortoli 'Sacred Hill' Semillon Sauvignon Blanc** as the *Quaff 2009* Best White Wine under $10.

CHARDONNAY

Although Marlborough sauvignon blanc has become the white drink of choice in restaurants and cafes throughout the country, followed by semillon sauvignon blanc blends, especially from Western Australia, chardonnay's position remains unchallenged. It's the most widely consumed Aussie white. Everyone says it's unpopular but someone is guzzling it.

It remains by far the most widely planted white wine grape in Australia – making up 44% of all the white wine grape vineyard area planted in Australia (32,000 hectares) and 18.5% of all vineyard plantings. In the past three years, plantings of chardonnay have slowed down and last year sauvignon blanc became the most planted white variety, followed by pinot gris and then chardonnay. However, last year 39,000 tonnes of sauvignon blanc were harvested and 13,000 tonnes of pinot gris/pinot grigio, compared with over 395,000 tonnes of chardonnay.

The figures for 2007 are much lower than 2006 and 2008 because of the drought. Chardonnay's closest white grape rivals are semillon (77,000 tonnes), colombard (61,000 tonnes), muscat gordo blanco (51,000 tonnes), followed by sauvignon blanc (up to 39,000 tonnes for the first time) ahead of riesling (33,000 tonnes). The shiraz crop was decimated in 2007 and so I wouldn't read anything into the fact that (for the first time) there was substantially more chardonnay harvested than shiraz (with only 293,000 tonnes).

The great strength of the Australian wine industry is its technological expertise and, in particular, its ability to produce large volumes of good to very good quality wine at reasonable prices. As a result, relatively few of the wines I have tasted for *Quaff* show winemaking faults. Many of those not reviewed lacked concentration of flavour, and appeared bland and dull. This may have occurred as a result of overcropping in the vineyard or sourcing the wines from very young vines.

Even in the last couple of vintages, there has been a significant reduction in the number of chardonnays that are too heavily oaked or show oak characters that are very charry or chippy. Clumsy winemaking, however, does mean that some whites have too much residual sugar and so appeared overly sweet. Australian chardonnays usually have a ripe fruit sweetness that is a large part of their popularity. There is a great difference between this fruit sweetness and sugar sweetness. Many chardonnays under $15 are softened and rounded out by a touch of residual sugar. Too much, however, spoils the balance of the wine and makes it taste syrupy or overly sweet on the finish.

Chardonnays which sell at $10 or below need to be sourced wholly, or in large part, from the warm to hot irrigated areas along the Murray River in South Australia, Victoria or New South Wales and on the Murrumbidgee in the Riverina. The best tend to be delicious, straightforward whites which rely on ripe fruit flavours for their easy drinkability. With careful viticulture and meticulous winemaking, it is possible to produce some of these wines in huge volumes without risking quality or consistency. In 2008, the Riverina had an outstanding vintage, helped by the ready availability (for a price) of water. Paul Lapsley, Chief Winemaker for Constellation, commented, 'Some of my highlights this year include Riverland chardonnays, with fine lemon flavours, avoiding the broader styles one might expect.' So you should find some terrific chardonnays from that region. Grapes from other parts of the Murray – in particular, Murray–Darling – have suffered from the drought and lack of water.

Chardonnays which sell for more than $10 are sourced, at least in part, from premium wine regions and from lower yielding vineyards. With more concentrated fruit, it is possible to use winemaking techniques which will produce more complex and therefore more interesting wines. These will be more full-bodied, have more weight, more richness, greater concentration and power.

The reliables –
consistent-quality wines, year in, year out

The most consistent chardonnay over the nine editions of *Quaff* has been McWilliams 'Hanwood' which, as one of the Reliables, has been omnipresent. It's a fantastic performance that, I believe, owes a great deal to the decision of the Chief Winemaker, Jim Brayne, to use 20–30% of fruit from premium areas to improve the flavour profile of the Riverina wine. At this price point, that strategy is a winner!

Buying and Drinking Chardonnay – Some Tips

Can chardonnay be unoaked?

There are certainly some who believe that without oak chardonnay is dull and bland or, at least, incapable of realising its potential. While I do think that clever or careful use of quality oak lifts chardonnay to new heights, there are always some excellent unwooded chardonnays reviewed in *Quaff*. At least those rated as 'Bloody Good' are fresh, clean and wonderfully youthful and – in quality terms – the equal of any (or almost any) wines in this chapter.

Zesty youth

One important difference between oaked and unoaked chardonnay is that the latter does rely on the first flush of youth for its vibrance and so is best within two years of vintage. Oaked chardonnay can be aged for a little bit longer. Having said that, most of the wines reviewed here are best drunk in the next 12 months – when their ripe fruit flavours will be at their freshest and most exuberant.

Unwooded Chardonnay

➤ BLOODY GOOD

2008 Capel Vale 'Debut' Unwooded Chardonnay $16.95

They are talking about it as perhaps the best-ever vintage in Western Australia, and looking at this wine, you could believe the claim. This is irresistible: lifted florals, ripe tropical fruit characters of passionfruit and guava, layer after layer of flavour moving towards a gentle crisp finish. Delicious.

2006 Leaping Lizard Unwooded Chardonnay $14.95

I'm surprised that this is still around and pleased that it tastes as good as it does. Sourced from Frankland River, as you'd expect for Ferngrove's second label, it is clean, powerful and full-bodied, still vibrant with rich, concentrated toasty melony flavours.

➤ GOOD

2007 Chapel Hill Unwooded Chardonnay $14

There's juicy ripe tropical flavours in this McLaren Vale white that is a bit leaner and crisper than I'd expect.

2007 Fishbone Unwooded Chardonnay $14.95

This popular label from Western Australia's unknown Blackwood Valley is fresh, clean and zippy with concentrated, rich, melony flavours, good mid-palate weight and a lively fruity finish.

2007 The Growers 'Peppermint Grove' Unwooded Chardonnay $14.95

There's a reasonable concentration of passionfruity flavours here in this multi-regional Western Australian white, plus a lively freshness and power.

2007 Taylors 'Promised Land' Unwooded Chardonnay $13.95

> Everyone knows the Clare Valley isn't a great place to grow chardonnay but, for the price, this is OK – well, good. It has some lifted perfumes, is fresh and lively with ripe, sweet tropical fruit, and a touch of sweetness to finish.

▬▶ PRETTY GOOD

2007 Angas Plains Unwooded Chardonnay $14.95

> Here's a pleasant, easy-drinking chardonnay from Langhorne Creek – fresh, clean and uncomplicated.

2007 Fox Creek 'Shadow's Run' Unwooded Chardonnay $12

> Much better to have a wine named after a dog than a cat, says Fling Forrestal, unequivocally. It has some tropical flavours, a juicy succulence and slightly sweet finish.

2007 Peos Unwooded Chardonnay $17.50

> From the West's truffle garden of Manjimup comes a pleasant, straightforward chardonnay that has ripe sweet fruit, is clean, crisp and fresh with some attractive sweetness.

Chardonnay

BLOODY GOOD

2007 Angoves 'Vineyard Select' Chardonnay $14.95

This is sourced from the southern Limestone Coast and has been treated with more care and thought than you'd normally find in a wine at this price. Much of it finished fermentation in French barriques and was lees stirred during maturation, while a small portion was made using natural yeast. It's fine, delicate and complex with peachy, melony flavours, creamy texture and a tight structure. Classy.

2007 Hardys 'Nottage Hill' Chardonnay $10.95

It's not often you hear the guys at Constellation express delight at their Nottage Hill Chardonnay – as they are with this vintage. It's mainly sourced from the Riverland with some Padthaway fruit adding a dimension to the flavour profile. There are some gentle, spicy oak aromas while the mid-palate is full flavoured and vibrant with intense, cool white peach tropical characters and a soft, pleasant finish.

2007 Houghton Chardonnay $14

There's plenty of value in the Houghton entry-level range. The more that the Western Australia winery pushes the boundaries with its more expensive chardonnays, the better this becomes. There are bright perfumes, ripe, sweet fruit of good intensity, all neatly balanced so that it lingers in the mouth.

2006 McWilliams 'Hanwood' Chardonnay $12

One of the Reliables – it has appeared in every edition of *Quaff* – the 2006 'Hanwood' Chardonnay looked impressive when I tried it last November and it was even better in August this year. As McWilliams has been doing for some time now, about 70% of this is sourced from the Riverina with the rest coming from the cooler Adelaide Hills, Eden Valley and Clare Valley, which alters the wine's profile, tightens its structure and gives it cooler, more intense flavour. It's quite lean, tight and powerful, nicely structured with good balance between oak and fruit, complex vanilla and grapefruit flavours, succulent, long and fine. Quaff on!

2007 Wolf Blass 'Yellow Label' Chardonnay $16.95

Look out for this on special as it's a cut above the 'Red Label' Chardonnay, There's a surprising complexity which reveals some interesting characters. It has an attractive mouthfeel, is dry, chalky and tangy, tightly structured, fine and precise. As you can see, there's a lot happening.

2007 Yering Station 'Mr Frog' Chardonnay $14.95

This shows that in the Yarra Valley even entry-level examples of the variety can make interesting drinking. It's soft, round and viscous with ripe concentrated cool-fruit flavour (think white peach, nectarine), creamy texture and some gentle cedary oak that is well integrated with the fruit.

 **GOOD**

2006 Bleasdale Chardonnay $14

A Langhorne Creek chardonnay that is exactly as you'd expect: slightly mellow, smooth texture, ripe sweet tropical flavours, quite sweet in the mid-palate yet lingering dry on the finish.

2007 Fifth Leg Chardonnay $20.95

I can't figure it out. I was talking to one of our major retailers who explained that his stores would have all the Fifth Leg wines available next week for $11 a bottle, and except when it's on special it'll be full price. It's a pretty funny system but that's the reason why I'm happy to feature the Devil's Lair wines in this section of *Quaff*. This is a refreshing regional Margaret River white with gentle oak, good mouthfeel, subtle but cool flavours.

2007 Gnangara Chardonnay $14

Part of the Evans & Tate portfolio but under the Gnangara label, signifying that it's sourced from around Western Australia. It has some cool green bean, snow pea flavours, good texture, balance and drinks soft and easy.

2007 Hardys 'Shuttles' Chardonnay (187 ml) $5

My samples came in tiny bottles with a plastic glass: obviously designed for picnics or outdoor consumption. Frankly, I don't approve. If this is a chink in my armour, I plead guilty. My view is that I want to taste or drink out of the best possible glass – even on a picnic. The wine was actually good – I tasted it out of our usual Riedel crystal glasses: ripe sweet peach flavours, lively mouthfeel, pleasing aftertaste. If you see it in big bottles without the plastic cups, I'd recommend it. If you see it in the small packs, and it suits, buy it, throw away the plastic cups, and use glass.

2008 McWilliams 'Hanwood' Crisp Chardonnay $12

The first vintage of this wine arrived too late for last year's *Quaff* but was featured on the website because I was so impressed. This is a new style for McWilliams, with some parcels of grapes picked earlier than usual to produce a lighter, fresher, zestier style. Interestingly, given its name, I used the word 'crisp' twice in my tasting notes when I had no idea what the wine was. This is fragrant, clean, crisp and fresh with lively, ripe, sweet peachy fruit and a crisp, zippy finish.

2007 Redbank 'Long Paddock' Chardonnay $13.95

This is a label of the Hill Smith family group and is sourced from the King Valley. It is clean, focused and attractive drinking, with ripe, sweet fruit and a nicely balanced finish.

2007 Sandalford 'Element' Chardonnay $14

There's plenty of cool tropical flavours (pineapple, peaches) in this finely balanced Western Australian white. It has a good mouthfeel and a refreshing, clean finish.

▄► PRETTY GOOD

2006 Acrobat Chardonnay $9.95

This chardonnay from Mudgee got strong support from one panel member, who enjoyed its rich, toasty characters. I was less enthusiastic yet enjoyed its freshness on the palate.

2007 Deakin Estate Chardonnay $10

A chardonnay from the Murray–Darling that is clean, crisp, fresh with a good mouthfeel and pleasant soft finish.

2007 De Bortoli 'Windy Peak' Chardonnay $15.20

An easy-drinking Victorian regional chardonnay that is straightforward but pleasant, highlighted with some fresh tropical flavours.

2007 McPherson Chardonnay $10.95

There's some ripe melony notes brightening up this fresh, clean white, plus an exuberant fruity finish.

2007 Tyrrells 'Midnight Leap' Chardonnay $11.95

Attractive fruity flavours that are clean and fresh and very easy to drink, in a wine that celebrates the late Murray Tyrrell's midnight leap into a vineyard to plunder some rare chardonnay vines from a neighbour. That was the beginning of Australia's love affair with chardonnay.

RIESLING

The popularity of riesling continues. One indicator of this was a rise in the volume of the variety harvested in 2006: up more than 25% on the 2003 crop. There was a drop-off in 2007 with the smallest harvest in years, riesling dropping about 20%, which was better than most varieties. The strong demand for premium riesling has resulted in an upward movement in the price of many of Australia's best quaffing rieslings; most Aussie rieslings sell for between $15 and $25 so you're seeing the best of the bargain-price rieslings in this chapter.

The reliables – consistent-quality wines, year in, year out

The rieslings from Peter Lehmann have appeared in all but one edition of *Quaff*. That's consistency!

Buying and Drinking Riesling – Some Tips

Drink young, fresh and vibrant
Most people enjoy rieslings when they are still in the first flush of youth (essentially within 18 months of harvest), when they are fragrant, fruity and lively with crisp dry acidity.

... or cellar for a few years
If you put riesling away in a cool dark place for a couple of years, it can develop some deliciously interesting bottle-age characters that are well worth exploring. Those with best cellaring potential include the 2008 Killihill Riesling, the 2008 Peter Lehmann Eden Valley Riesling and the 2008 Thorn Clarke 'Sandpiper' Riesling.

Rejoice in screwcaps
The wholesale move away from cork – triggered in many ways by the united force of the Clare Valley's riesling producers, who made a bold statement by rejecting cork en masse and moving to screwcap closures – has changed the face of the Australian wine industry. Cork taint, a dominant issue for wine writers and a major problem for the industry, has been dramatically reduced as the percentage of bottles sealed with cork decreases. As long as it's well cellared, riesling will age much better under screwcap.

Unfashionable value
As we say plenty of times in other parts of the book, if a wine is unfashionable expect it to be cheap. Although riesling is more fashionable than it was a few years ago, it is still unfashionable except with wine lovers. It represents amazing value – mainly thanks to the popularity of sauvignon blanc, sem sauv blancs and chardonnay.

▶ BLOODY GOOD

2007 Angoves 'Vineyard Select' Riesling $14.95

This is from a single vineyard in the Watervale area of Clare and was highly recommended last year. It's bold, powerful and concentrated with dense limey-lemony flavours and some toasty notes. There's still zesty taut acidity to finish.

2008 Kirrihill Riesling $18

This is a very impressive riesling from a single vineyard in Watervale. I have spoken to the guys at Kirrihill about this Single Vineyard Series as they have given each of the wines a Gaelic name. This is called 'Cuaisín na Sléine'. I suspect that they want you to remember that name and ask for it next time you're in your favourite retailer's store. Not my idea of bright marketing. The wine itself is terrific: a hint of talc aroma, bold lemon citrus and lime juice flavours that are rich and concentrated, power yet balance and a lemony tang on a finish of some length.

2008 Peter Lehmann Eden Valley Riesling $16.50

The previous vintage was the *Quaff 2008* Wine of the Year and this riesling is consistently among the best-value wines on the planet. As it is this year. There's power and intensity of lime juice and lemongrass flavours yet the wine has delicacy, subtlety and finesse before its dry, crisp finish leaves you asking for more.

2008 Thorn Clarke 'Sandpiper' Riesling $14.95

The Sandpiper label has done extraordinarily well for Thorn Clarke in this year's *Quaff* and this is arguably the best wine in the range. It is juicy, even succulent, subtle, delicate and fine, with intense lemon citrus flavours that build in the glass before a fresh, dry, zesty finish. Not surprisingly, it is sourced from the Thorn Clarke vineyards high in the Barossa Ranges.

2006 Vintage Cellars Eden Valley Riesling $11.95

This shows the benefits of carefully ageing Australian riesling – there's a hint of development without any loss of freshness. There are some toasty characters on the nose, fresh nutty, lemon curd flavours of good intensity and lively zippy acid. Exclusive to Vintage Cellars.

 **GOOD**

2008 Cookoothama Riesling $14.95

A light, fine, delicate riesling from Nugan Estate's King Valley vineyard. There are abundant intense lemon citrus flavours and a crisp, clean finish.

2007 De Bortoli 'Sacred Hill' Riesling $6.60

This cheapie has very soft acidity which makes it somewhat unriesling-like. I think there's plenty to like here: its clean, focused lime juice flavours, softness in the mid-palate and reasonably intense finish.

2007 De Bortoli 'Windy Peak' Riesling $15.20

This is gentler than many rieslings and may have wide appeal: it is soft, round and easy to drink with lemon citrus flavours and a finish that is clean, fresh and zesty.

2008 Peter Lehmann Barossa Valley Riesling $13.95

While this doesn't have the power or grunt of the Eden Valley wines, it's still pretty impressive. There's a pleasing juiciness, lighter body yet with some intensity of lemon citrus flavours, fruit purity that is a key to my enjoyment of riesling, before a fresh, clean, fine finish that lingers.

2008 Richard Hamilton 'Slate Quarry' Riesling $13.95

A McLaren Vale riesling with lemon citrus flavours and zesty acidity.

◖▬ PRETTY GOOD

2007 Hardys 'Nottage Hill' Riesling $10.50

> While this is restrained on the nose, it is clean and focused with bright lemongrass and lime flavours, plump and fleshy with zippy acidity to finish.

2008 Jim Barry Watervale Riesling $14.95

> This appears a bit lighter than usual, still with the finesse you'd expect of the excellent Clare winery: lemony, fresh and good drinking.

2008 Logan 'Weemala' Riesling $15.95

> A powerful riesling from high (at 1000 metres) on the slopes of Mt Canobolas in the Orange region. It has strong lemony flavours and questionably fierce acidity.

2007 Long Flat 'Destinations' Riesling $14.95

> Here is a pleasant Clare Valley riesling under the Long Flat regional series. It's quite soft and easy to drink with some lemon drop characters and a gentle finish.

2006 Two Churches Riesling $11.95

> The Vintage Cellars Barossa label offers a riesling that shows hints of toastiness and citrus blossom on the nose and then powerful lime juice and lemon citrus flavours. The finish is the question mark: if you like bold acidity you'll be fine. Some of the panel found it searing. Exclusive to Vintage Cellars.

SAUVIGNON BLANC

Sauvignon is the trendy grape variety as Aussies continue their love affair and sales rise – especially in the cafes, bistros and brasseries. The Kiwis are doing amazing business over here, especially with their Marlborough sauvignons, which are well-nigh impossible to beat at the price. Talk about fruit bombs! You should hear the Aussie wine marketers talk about Kiwis and their sauvignon blanc.

Australia's best sauvignon blancs tend to come from our cooler wine regions (where yields are lower and costs higher) and most of these are priced between $17 and $25, and creeping up. The best areas include the Adelaide Hills, Orange, Tasmania, the Alpine Valleys, the Grampians, Padthaway, (the south of) Margaret River and the Great Southern.

There are plenty of lacklustre or bland sauvignon blancs on the market in the under-$15 price bracket. These tend to be clean and fresh yet lack clear varietal character or concentration of flavour. Those rated 'Bloody Good' and 'Good' are light and bright with intense varietal flavours – even interest and excitement – and I'm delighted to be able to recommend them.

The reliables –
consistent-quality wines, year in, year out

The Westend 'Richland' is one of the Reliables, having been reviewed in each edition of *Quaff*. It's a stunning performance as most of the other Riverina, or indeed warm area, sauvignons lack intensity and concentration of flavour. Better still, this is an outstanding vintage for the 'Richland' Sauvignon Blanc, possibly the best ever.

Buying and Drinking Sauvignon Blanc – A Tip

Fresh and lively
The deadline for tastings has been kept as late as practical in the year to make it possible for wineries to present the current harvest's offerings. The pattern in *Quaff* has been for this chapter to be dominated by the most recent vintage, as it is this year. As a general rule, sauvignon blanc is a variety for drinking while it's fresh, young and lively.

BLOODY GOOD

 2008 Westend 'Richland' Sauvignon Blanc $10.95
THE QUAFF 2009 'Utterly Delectable'
WHITE WINE OF THE YEAR AWARD
We tend to be keen to salute our *Quaff* champions – like this superbly consistent, style-breaking white from the Riverina. It has spent the best part of a decade (nine years) as one of the Reliables. There's an added dimension of complexity to the 2008 Richland Sauvignon Blanc that makes it more than a delicious drink. There are green bean and green pepper characters on the nose and palate with some complexing gunflint, smoky notes. It's lean, tightly structured with zesty acidity adding a refreshing quality on the finish.

2008 Yalumba 'Mawsons' Sauvignon Blanc $15.95
This is sourced from Wrattonbully and is very impressive at the price. It's delightfully fragrant, has cool tropical flavours, is vibrant and tangy in the mid-palate and finishes clean and dry.

2008 Yalumba 'Y Series' Sauvignon Blanc $12.95
While the Mawsons is taut and tangy, this 'Y Series' Sauvignon is riper, softer and sweeter, showing flavours of pineapple and passionfruit in abundance before a crisp, clean finish.

GOOD

2008 Angoves 'Long Row' Sauvignon Blanc $9.95
There's an intriguing character on the nose of fresh herbs ('lemon myrtle' said one panel member, 'peppermint' claimed another. Fascinating, I thought). It's bright and vibrant, a little lacking in concentration but a pleasing drink.

2008 De Bortoli 'Deen Vat 2' Sauvignon Blanc $12.95

The good year for the Riverina comes through in this lively white: grassy, green-skinned fruit characters with ripe, sweet tropical flavours, balanced by zippy acidity.

2007 Saltram 'Makers Table' Sauvignon Blanc $10.95

Saltram is a great Barossa label (although Makers Table is one of the silliest names ever for a range of wines) and this is a terrific, well-priced sauvignon: some grassy flavours, almost a touch of snow pea and green bean and a clean, zesty, vibrant finish.

2007 Scarpantoni 'Pedler Creek' Sauvignon Blanc $14

I'd be hunting in the nearby Adelaide Hills for more expensive, tighter, tauter sauvignon – and thus miss out on this well-priced McLaren Vale sauvignon blanc. You should be pleased that Scarpantoni is in control. This is fresh and lively with full ripe flavours, good viscous texture and a crisp balanced finish. Easy drinking.

 PRETTY GOOD

2007 McGuigan 'Black Label' Sauvignon Blanc $9.95

A pleasant easy-drinking sauvignon blanc made for everyday drinking.

2008 McWilliams 'Hanwood' Sauvignon Blanc $12.95

This is bright and juicy with ripe tropical flavours and a soft, easy finish.

2007 Rex Watson Sauvignon Blanc $14.95

Here's a Coonawarra white from a new company that is making an impression, especially with its budget-priced wines. This is clean, fresh and lively with ripe sweet tropical flavours. Easy to like.

SEMILLON

This is a tiny section, mainly due to the decline in the number of semillons we are seeing for less than $15 a bottle. Australia is still producing heaps of semillon: it is second only to chardonnay in terms of volume of the variety produced (77,000 tonnes in the below-average yields of 2007) and way ahead of sauvignon blanc and riesling. However, the success of semillon sauvignon blanc as an everyday drinking style means that that blend is much easier to market than varietal semillon.

As a varietal white, semillon is unique to Australia. The style of wine that it produces differs dramatically depending on the part of the country in which it is grown. In New South Wales' Hunter Valley it is a world-class wine that ages brilliantly. Lean, dry and often austere while young, it develops into a mellow, toasty, honeyed classic with time in the bottle. Interestingly, the Hunter vignerons are working hard at reinventing themselves and semillon, and are looking to produce a more attractive, more marketable young wine than ever before. There's not much Hunter Valley semillon on the market under $15 but there are great examples here from Tulloch and Tyrrells.

In South Australia's Barossa Valley, semillon produces richer, fuller wines with more lemony flavours. In recent times, more wineries in this region have been moving away from oaked semillons and are making fresher, livelier, more drink-now styles. Western Australia's Margaret River and Great Southern produce a fresh, herbal, green-pea, green-bean style of semillon that has many admirers. The vast majority of these wines sell for more than $15 or are blended with sauvignon blanc to make a fresh, easy drink-now white blend, which is the only challenger to New Zealand sauvignon in cafes, brasseries and restaurants.

The following may be a tiny selection, but the wines reviewed are impressive.

The reliables –
consistent-quality wines, year in, year out

The Hunter Valley's Tyrrells and the Barossa's Peter Lehmann have been the leading producers of quaffing semillon and have been reviewed in eight of the nine editions of this annual guide.

Buying and Drinking Semillon – A Tip

Each-way bets

One of the great things about semillon – especially from the Hunter Valley – is that it can be enjoyed while young for its fresh, lively youthfulness or cellared for five to seven years and enjoyed for its mellow, toasty, honeyed flavours. Of the wines reviewed here, I think the Tulloch, the Tyrrells and the Peter Lehmann have the best ageing potential.

▶ BLOODY GOOD

2006 Peter Lehmann Semillon $13.50

This iconic Hunter Valley label makes huge volumes of first-rate Barossa semillon and is finding it harder than usual to sell because of our current obsession with Marlborough sauvignon. Followers of *Quaff* benefit in a couple of ways. The wine ages beautifully so the fact that this is from the 2006 vintage is not a problem: it's certainly as fresh as it has ever been. And the price of this wine is kept low. For many years now, the Peter Lehmann Semillon has seen no wood and it benefits from that by showing pure lemon citrus flavours of good intensity and power, a mid-palate tang, and a zingy dry finish that lingers.

2008 Tulloch Semillon $16

One of the great Hunter Valley wine families appears to be thriving – certainly they are making some excellent wines. This has some attractive sweet pea and sugar snap pea flavours, is vibrant and fresh before a clean, zesty finish.

2006 Two Churches Semillon $11.95

This is a Vintage Cellars label from the Barossa Valley that over delivers on price. There are some attractive toasty characters, fine, delicate yet concentrated lemon citrus flavours, all delightfully viscous before a refreshingly dry finish that lingers. Exclusive to Vintage Cellars.

▶ GOOD

2007 Tyrrells 'Old Winery' Semillon $13.95

Tyrrells is one of the Hunter Valley's great semillon producers, with good value at a range of prices. This is the entry-level wine. It shows some attractive talc aromas, sherberty, lemon citrus flavours, is neatly balanced, fresh and pristine with a crisp, zesty dry finish.

OTHER WHITE VARIETALS

The most popular varieties submitted for this section were verdelho, pinot grigio (and pinot gris) and viognier. Pinot grigio is the flavour of the month: it sells brilliantly in cafes, brasseries and restaurants and is being planted in substantially increased amounts. At a time when there has been negative growth with most white varieties, pinot gris increased by 83% from 2006 to 2007 and viognier by 33% (although in both cases this is from a small base). There are now only 2469 hectares of pinot grigio/gris in total, and 1369 hectares of viognier. Interestingly, there are plenty of pinot grigios in the under $15 price bracket but fewer viogniers, for which you usually have to pay more. The key to understanding pinot gris and pinot grigio is that these are textural wines with little obvious varietal fruit characters – very much savoury rather than fruity whites, with the best of them finishing dry. Because of this they are excellent food wines.

Verdelho, by contrast, tends to be very fruity and easy to enjoy without thinking very much. No wonder it's popular.

The reliables –
consistent-quality wines, year in, year out

After nine editions of *Quaff*, only two wines have appeared in this section on each occasion: the Moondah Brook Verdelho and the Tahbilk Marsanne – consistently excellent value-for-money wines. The price of the Moondah Brook, along with pretty much everything in the Hardys portfolio, has gone up by a couple of dollars. I'm confident that it should be available on discount for less than $15 but will monitor the situation before next year's *Quaff*. I suspect that next year it will go the way of several other Reliables that have crept out of our price bracket.

Buying and Drinking Other White Varietals – A Tip

Fresh is best

As usual, this chapter is dominated by whites from the most recent vintage. These tend to be unwooded and rely on freshness. Their vitality and ripe, full-on flavour are very much part of the joy that the best of these wines can impart.

BLOODY GOOD

2008 Angoves 'Long Row' Verdelho $9.95

There's a lot to like about this vibrant varietal. It has floral aromas with a touch of talc, soft, round, concentrated, ripe, sweet tropical flavours, a hint of musk, and a lingering aftertaste.

2007 Brown Brothers Vermentino $16.95

I fell in love with this bright, refreshing Sardinian varietal on a media trip to Italy, when I took every opportunity to try as many different examples of it as possible. There are a few in Australia at present, with more on the way – and we're doing pretty well with the variety. This is fresh, clean and vibrantly fruity with a characteristic bitter almond finish that cleanses the palate.

2008 Capel Vale 'Debut' Verdelho $16.95

The Western Australia verdelho style is different from that of the Hunter: the flavours tend to be more overtly fruity and the wines exuberant and less textured, relying on the burst of full-throttle flavour. In the excellent 2008 vintage, Capel Vale provides an exemplary sample of what the West can do: it's ripe and gentle with intense sweet tropical fruits such as passionfruit and guava, fine and delicate and delicious easy drinking. Quaff on!

2007 De Bortoli 'Windy Peak' Viognier $14.95

It's been another brilliant year for the Victorian Windy Peak label. What impresses most about this viognier is the purity of its varietal fruit. It presents fresh and clean with pleasing viscosity and lively, zippy acidity.

2008 Logan 'Weemala' Gewurztraminer $15.95

Logan is based in Mudgee and sources fruit from there and the cooler, higher region of Orange. It's back-to-back triumphs with this gewurztraminer: riotously aromatic, grapey, rose-petal flavours that are long, clean and fresh with a zippy dry finish.

2008 Logan 'Weemala' Pinot Gris $15.95

The wine is sourced from two vineyards in Orange – one at 650 metres and the other at 1000 metres – so they produce ultra-cool grapes. Buckets of rain in February ruined the Hunter vintage but a dry windy spell in March meant that the vintage in Orange did not suffer. The Pinot Gris has a pink tinge, is gently fragrant, has refreshing cool flavours with a savoury edge and a pleasing dry finish.

2008 Tahbilk Marsanne $14.90

The omnipresent, ever-reliable Tahbilk Marsanne is sourced from a single vineyard in Nagambie Lakes which represents the world's largest planting of marsanne. It's one of the *Quaff* Reliables, present in every edition of the guide. I prefer the current vintage to the good 2007, for its clean, lightly tropical and grassy notes, intensity of flavour and refreshingly zesty, dry finish.

2008 Tulloch Verdelho $16.00

These are good days for this revitalised Hunter Valley winery and this is a much better verdelho than you'll find at most of the region's cellar doors. There are some beguiling florals, soft, round, ripe sweet fruity flavours with a touch of rose petal, more depth than usual and a better mouthfeel; finesse too. The lingering aftertaste also delights.

2007 Wyndham Estate 'Bin 111' Verdelho $14.95

This is a very impressive Hunter Valley verdelho that appears to build layer after layer of ripe sweet tropical fruit (guava, lychees, passionfruit) so that it floods the palate. Even with a year of bottle age, it's bright, fresh, spotlessly clean – and delicious.

2007 Zilzie Viognier $14.95

The warmth of regions like the Murray–Darling is proving to be admirably suitable to this northern Rhône variety – without perhaps the concentration that the French get when the vines are perched perpendicularly overlooking the River Rhône. There are some rose-petal aromas, good viscosity, rich full flavours and a lively balanced finish.

 **GOOD**

2008 McWilliams 'Hanwood' Pinot Gris $12.95

Another of the Riverina wines to show up the excellent 2008 vintage in the region. It's particularly attractive on the palate, where its soft, silky smooth viscosity makes for such easy drinking, while its lingering dry finish means that it'll be a nice match for food – even the weekly fish and chips.

2008 Moondah Brook Verdelho $18

One of the Reliables, omnipresent in *Quaff* for its first nine editions: price may drive this out of the list of Reliables next year. The Moondah Brook range tends to be available on special for less than $15 quite readily. There's heaps of ripe sweet fruit nicely concentrated, thanks to the excellent 2008 vintage in Western Australia. It's quite tight in the mid-palate with vibrant tangy flavours and a zesty finish.

2007 Peel Estate Premium White $14.95

This is made from chenin blanc and is clean and fresh with some limey, fruity flavours. While not greatly concen-trated, it is neatly balanced and a good drink.

2007 Thorn Clarke 'Sandpiper' Pinot Gris $14.95

A pleasant easy-to-like Barossa white that has some savoury characters which give a good mouthfeel, and a refreshing, cleansing finish.

2008 Upper Reach 'Black Bream' $14.95

How clever is this? It is the entry-level white for one of the Swan Valley's top producers and is made from 100% chenin blanc. Now I acknowledge that chenin makes great wine in the Loire Valley and better whites than anything much except verdelho in the Swan Valley. But I'm not a fan. I tasted this and liked it and have only just found out it was chenin. The 'Black Bream' is intensely fruity with ripe tropical flavours, and is tangy, zesty and even exuberant.

2008 Westend 'Richland' Pinot Grigio $10.95

This Riverina varietal is nicely aromatic with clean, fresh, restrained fruit flavours but being more savoury and dry, in the style of pinot grigio. An attractive food wine.

2008 Yalumba 'Y Series' Pinot Grigio $12.95

This is a subtle, neatly balanced white that has attractive fruity aromas, pleasing viscosity and savoury flavours before a long, dry finish. As a variety, pinot grigio/pinot gris calls to be drunk with fresh, light-bodied dishes.

2007 Yalumba 'Y Series' Viognier $11.95

As usual, this is a subtle, delicate white that relies on its balance for its impact. Here ripe, sweet fruit is balanced by a zesty refreshing acidity.

◀ PRETTY GOOD

2008 Angoves 'Nine Vines' Pinot Grigio $14

This Riverland pinot grigio is soft, round, and attractive current drinking thanks to its savoury characters and lingering dry finish. Try it with a Vietnamese stir-fry chicken dish.

2008 De Bortoli 'Windy Peak' Pinot Grigio $14.95

> Clean, fresh and well made, restrained and pleasant easy drinking.

2007 McGuigan 'Black Label' Verdelho $9.95

> While this is a bit lacking in concentration of flavour, it's soft and slips down all too well.

2008 McWilliams 'Hanwood' Verdelho $12.95

> There's heaps of ripe sweet fruit flavours here, a touch of sweetness to flesh it out in the mid-palate and on the finish: a pleasant quaffer.

2008 Redbank 'Long Paddock' Pinot Grigio $13.95

> There's all the zestiness of the cool King Valley climate packed in here in this straightforward, easy-drinking style with noticeable acidity to finish.

2008 Tyrrells 'Old Winery' Verdelho $13.95

> An entry-point label for Tyrrells that offers attractive drinking at a good price. This has ripe tropical fruit flavours and is uncomplicated summery quaffing.

SEMILLON SAUVIGNON BLANC BLENDS

Some of the pioneers of the Margaret River region experimented with this style in the early 1980s, it was popularised in the 1990s and since then has made a huge impact on the Australian scene. Its vibrance and drinkability have made it a huge favourite. The tsunami of Marlborough sauvignon blanc in recent years has slowed down the progress of sem sauv blancs, but not much.

Semillon from Margaret River has a grassy character that bears an amazing resemblance to sauvignon blanc, more so than from other areas. Combining the two varieties seemed a natural thing to do as the weight, full body and complexity of semillon added a dimension to the vibrant juiciness of sauvignon blanc. The blend was a much more immediately satisfying drink than either of the two components. Because of its popularity and cost of production, most of the good examples of the blend from Margaret River have moved above $15 a bottle and their place has been taken by producers in the cooler areas of Western Australia – especially Pemberton and Frankland River – where the grapes are cheaper and, in many cases, zingier.

The important thing about this blend is having a fresh, zesty sauvignon blanc component. Many producers will get this by sourcing sauvignon blanc (or at least some of it) from a cool region. Those who rely on fruit from a warmer region will usually pick it early to retain the lively acidity that adds sparkle to the blend.

The popularity of the blend has led to imitators throughout the country. Some are very smart wines. Others are very reasonably priced, as you'll see among those recommended in this chapter.

The reliables –
consistent-quality wines, year in, year out

The Houghton Semillon Sauvignon Blanc has been in seven of the nine editions of *Quaff* and is back in after being released too late to make the book last year. In a role reversal, the Plantagenet 'Hazard Hill' Semillon Sauvignon Blanc – also featured in seven editions of *Quaff* – has been released too late to make the book this year, even though the winemakers (or was it the marketing department?) promised we'd have it. When they are available both wines are consistently good value. Willow Bridge has repeated its 'Bloody Good' rating from last year and is so impressive that it's worth making a song and dance about.

Buying and Drinking Semillon Sauvignon Blanc Blends – A Tip

A quaffing good drink

I'm a great believer in drinking wines over a meal and there are plenty of light, uncomplicated dishes that are suited to accompanying semillon sauvignon blanc blends – summery salads, creamy pastas, Asian noodles and Chinese stir-fries, especially those made with seafood or chicken. There will be times, however, when you may well want to relax with a refreshing glass of wine – on a quiet summer's afternoon or at a rowdy Friday night party – and this light, bright blend offers plenty of choice.

◗ BLOODY GOOD

2007 Cartwheel Semillon Sauvignon Blanc $15.95

> Here is a merchant label of Fosters to give it another Western Australian sem sauv blanc in its portfolio, especially for restaurants. There are restrained yet concentrated cool, white peach flavours, a pleasant mouthfeel and crisp, zesty acidity.

★ 2008 De Bortoli 'Sacred Hill' Semillon Sauvignon Blanc $7.50

> THE QUAFF 2009 'Light, Bright and Easy'
> BEST WHITE WINE UNDER $10 AWARD
> This is a revelation – a delicious quaffing white at a bargain-basement price. It's soft, round and juicy, almost fleshy, with ripe tropical fruit flavours that are youthful, fresh and bright.

2008 Kirrihill 'Companions' Semillon Sauvignon Blanc $14.95

> The Companions range has done extraordinarily well for Kirrihill this year and helps to emphasise the Clare Valley's credentials for budget-priced wines. This combines the full flavour of ripe tropicals with an impressive textural feel; a soft, attractive mouthfeel and crisp, dry finish.

2008 Logan 'Apple Tree Flat' Semillon Sauvignon Blanc $11

> Every now and then the consistent Logan pulls one out of the hat for this entry-level label. There are powerful green bean, grassy flavours that persist, a pleasing crunchiness before a zesty dry finish. Some might find it confronting but it's an appealing style.

2008 Willow Bridge Sauvignon Blanc Semillon $15.50

Situated in the stunningly picturesque Ferguson Valley (in the Geographe region) with fabulous hillside views over the hinterland towards the coastal town of Bunbury, Willow Bridge is making crackingly good SBS blends. This is a stunner. It has bright, lifted aromatics, intense gooseberry, guava and pineapple tropical flavours, a vibrant, succulent mouthfeel and spellbinding natural acidity, finishing fresh, clean and long.

2007 Xanadu 'Dragon' Sauvignon Blanc Semillon $16

Glenn Goodall and the team at Rathbone's Xanadu, close to the township of Margaret River, have well and truly re-established the credentials of the winery so this wine doesn't surprise. It's fresh, clean and lively with apple and grapefruit flavours, plus some ripe tropical notes and strong zesty acidity.

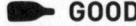 **GOOD**

2008 Calder Grove Semillon Sauvignon Blanc $15.95

This is from Ilrymple in the Murray–Darling and benefits from being picked early. There's lively youthful sugar snap pea flavours, some depth of flavour before a vibrant zesty finish.

2008 De Bortoli 'Montage' Semillon Sauvignon Blanc $9.95

There's plenty to like about this white blend – and not just the price. It's ripe and peachy, soft and round, has a good mouthfeel and a refreshing finish.

2007 Houghton Sauvignon Blanc Semillon $14

At last my brother's favourite, this consistently good WA white blend, is sealed with screwcaps. No more grumbles about corked wines. The 2007 is more restrained, delicate and subtle than usual: the flavour is there, it just needs time to open up.

2007 Long Flat Semillon Sauvignon Blanc $9.95

This is lifted by a plump, fleshy character on the mid-palate that ensures a pleasing mouthfeel before a soft, easy finish.

2008 Miles from Nowhere Sauvignon Blanc Semillon $14.95

This is the first vintage I've seen from the Margaret River vineyard of former Evans & Tate owner, Franklin Tate (it's close to Howard Park in Wilyabrup). There's quality fruit, plenty of green bean, fresh garden herb flavours and a finish that is clean and crisp. The price is right, too.

2008 Peter Lehmann 'Clancy's' Semillon Sauvignon Blanc $14.95

There's certainly value here in this Barossa white blend: it's soft and round with ripe tropical flavours and a fresh, clean finish that lingers. Easy drinking.

 PRETTY GOOD

2008 Angoves 'Brightlands' Sauvignon Blanc Semillon $14.95

This is a soft, round easy-drinking white blend under a new label for Angoves. There's some passionfruit flavours and very gentle acidity.

2008 Capel Vale 'Debut' Sauvignon Blanc Semillon $16.95

While this lacks the concentration of some of the Capel Vale whites, it's well made, soft, round and very easy to drink.

2008 Four Sisters Sauvignon Blanc Semillon $14.30

This is attractive drinking: floral aromas, crunchy tropical fruit that is fresh and lively before a zesty finish.

2007 Grant Burge 'Barossa Vines' Semillon Sauvignon Blanc $16.30

This is an easy-drinking Barossa white with less obvious flavour yet good length.

2007 Hardys 'Nottage Hill' Semillon Sauvignon Blanc $10.50

> This is tighter, leaner and cooler than usual, with more restrained flavours that finish fresh and lively.

2008 Leaping Lizard Semillon Sauvignon Blanc $14

> This is the second label of Frankland River's Ferngrove. It is brightened by green pea characters and is a very easy-drinking style. Some will find it a bit soft on the finish.

2008 McWilliams 'Hanwood' Semillon Sauvignon Blanc $12.95

> There's attractive green-skinned fruit here, fresh clean and lively with zippy dry acidity.

2007 Poet's Corner Semillon Sauvignon Blanc $9.95

> There's good intensity here with some grassy, herby characters and a lively, zippy finish.

2008 Talinga Park Semillon Sauvignon Blanc $9.95

> Here's an easy-drinking white blend from the Riverina that won't break the bank.

OTHER WHITE BLENDS

I said it last year and I'm saying it again. I found the tasting for this chapter pretty hard work. The fact of the matter is that because of the price point that is being targeted, these are blended bin-end wines. So everything goes into the blend – and I get to taste the most amazing combinations imaginable. The bonus is that, although the tasting (overall) was disappointing, the top wines were once again terrific.

Especially in this chapter, blind tastings are a significant part of *Quaff*. As I don't know what the blends are until after I have finished making notes on the wines and rating them, I can't be put off by my expectations of what a seemingly bizarre combination of grapes might produce. Surprise packets to impress include the 2008 Primo Estate 'La Biondina' Colombard Sauvignon Blanc, 2008 De Bortoli 'Sero' Chardonnay Pinot Grigio (both backing up on success last year) and the 2008 Kirrihill 'Companions' Riesling Pinot Gris.

Thank goodness Australian appellation laws allow for blending literally any grape from anywhere with any other grape from anywhere else. What is pleasing, too, is that these blends still express a good sense of where they're from – whether it be the grassy, fresh, perfumed quality of the Western Australian blends or the ripe, rich flavours of the warmer-climate South Australian wines.

An increased number of producers are avoiding saying what the blends are – which is often a great idea. If people like the wine, what does it matter what's in it? At least, that would be how the wine-maker's argument would go.

For the second year there will be no Semillon Chardonnay section: with only four wines reviewed here that's no loss. With the popularity of semillon sauvignon blanc blends, winemakers are not prepared to sacrifice semillon for the fairly unfashionable sem chardonnays and so this category has all but disappeared from retailers' shelves.

The reliables –
consistent-quality wines, year in, year out

Only one wine in this section has appeared in all nine editions of *Quaff* – the Primo Estate 'La Biondina' Colombard Sauvignon Blanc. 'La Biondina' has moved to this section from Other White Varietals – where it shone as a straight colombard. In 2004 and 2005 it was labelled a blend of colombard, sauvignon blanc and riesling and now it's colombard sauvignon blanc.

Buying and Drinking Other White Blends – Some Tips

Fresh is best

There is no question that the fresher these blends are the better they are. With one exception, all these wines are either from 2007 or 2008. They need to be drunk before they are two years old, while their fruit flavours are at their liveliest and brightest. In fact, they are generally at their best before they have had their first birthday.

Summertime blues

The best of these blends make great uncomplicated summertime drinking and are now being sourced from many parts of Australia rather than, as previously, along the banks of the mighty River Murray. This variety in the places from which they are sourced means that you have greater choice in the styles you drink than before. If you want a dry white blend, it's available.

BLOODY GOOD

2007 Cuttlefish Classic White $14

Here is the well-performed second label of Margaret River contract winemaker, Flying Fish Cove, which has its own vineyards and labels. This blend of sauvignon blanc, semillon and chardonnay is lightly floral and has intense green bean, green pea and fresh garden herb flavours, finishing crisp and lively.

2008 De Bortoli 'Sero' Chardonnay Pinot Grigio $14.20

Sourced, like all in the Sero range, from the cool King Valley, this is a bit lacking in concentration yet is fresh, clean and vibrant with a good mouthfeel and crisp, zesty finish.

2007 Hamelin Bay 'Rampant White' Semillon Sauvignon Blanc Chardonnay $18

Here's another Margaret River winery with a blend of sauvignon blanc, semillon and chardonnay: this time from the region's deep south where the white grapes love the cool. I particularly like the fact that this is less sweet than many of these white blends. Intense snow pea and green bean flavours are persistent before a clean, refreshing, dry finish.

2008 Kirrihill 'Companions' Riesling Pinot Gris $13.50

An unusual blend but one that works well for this Clare Valley winery that has performed particularly well in this year's *Quaff*. It's good drinking: juicy, fresh and succulent with some pear flavour and a crisp, clean finish.

2008 Primo Estate 'La Biondina' Colombard Sauvignon Blanc $14.95

This is absolutely fabulous – almost good enough for me to forgive Joe Grilli for the exhilarating drive in his Maserati (he is a very good driver, which is just as well). Who says wine writers don't occasionally have fun? On a more serious note, if you're in McLaren Vale (and why wouldn't you be?) make sure to call into Primo Estate – it's on my list of the country's best half-dozen cellar doors. Back to the wine: this a great vintage for 'La Biondina', vibrant grassy flavours that zip and zing across the palate, multidimensional and tangy with a pristine dry finish that refreshes.

2007 Swings & Roundabouts 'Kiss Chasey' Premium White $14.95

A well-priced Margaret River white that has been fleshed out in the mid-palate by some fruity sweetness. It is bound to have appeal because of its grassy, tropical flavours and zesty finish.

 **GOOD**

2007 De Bortoli 'Sacred Hill' Semillon Chardonnay $7.50

There's plenty of fruity flavour here – lively grassy flavours – good balance and a clean lively finish that lingers.

2007 Fishbone Classic White $14.95

A clever label that relies on its Western Australian origins although it consistently delivers: there's plenty of weight of lively nectarine fruit, good viscosity and layers of flavour.

2007 Houghton Chardonnay Verdelho $14

I remember current Constellation Chief Winemaker Paul Lapsley, when he was at Houghton, causing a stir by putting these two varieties together. That was a decade or more ago and the style still does well for Houghton. Certainly, the chardonnay seems to give verdelho much-needed structure without detracting from its strong primary flavours. This is clean and vibrant with pleasing intensity before a zesty crisp finish.

2007 Houghton White Classic $14

> At last the Houghton White Burgundy (HWB) with its silly undignified new name is under screwcap. The wine is as good as ever, just a bit more restrained than usual. Normally it's quite exuberant as a young wine. I found this more textural, subtler and more delicate. I needed to stop and think about it, appreciate the wine to get the most enjoyment out of it. If you're a fan of the wine – and I am – buy it. It's every bit as good as usual, just needs a bit of understanding.

2007 Lamonts Quartet $13.50

> This is an improbable blend of verdelho, chardonnay, chenin blanc and semillon from one of the Swan Valley's top producers: it is well made, youthful, lively and with plenty of characters before a refreshing zesty finish.

2008 Lindemans 'Early Harvest' Crisp Dry White $13.95

> Picking early certainly works well for this attractive blend: it's clean, fresh and lively with pleasing juiciness in the mid-palate and plenty of zest and zing to finish.

2007 Pikes 'White Mullet' $14.95

> An unlikely Clare Valley blend of riesling, viognier and chenin blanc results in a fresh, juicy white showing some apple and pear flavours and cleansing zippy acidity.

2008 Rosemount Estate 'Diamond Cellars' Traminer Riesling $11.95

> A good example of this sweet style: it's aromatic with some talc and floral notes, has pleasant, sweet grapey flavours and a sweet finish that avoids being cloying.

2007 Victorian Alps Dividing Range Sauvignon Blanc Colombard Chardonnay $10

> It's hard to complain of a cool-climate blend, even if it is the unlikely mix of sauvignon blanc, colombard and chardonnay. There are some cool white peach flavours and a decent mouthfeel: it's relaxed easy drinking.

2006 Western Range 'Old Well' Classic White $9

This is a budget-priced range from the Perth Hills producer. It's older than I'd want but still drinking pleasantly.

Willespie 'River Pearl' $14.95

Willespie is one of the grand old Margaret River names – established by Kevin and Marion Squance in 1976. They're fabulously situated in Wilyabrup and one of my friends had a great experience at the cellar door recently. They've been pretty quiet for some time and I've heard that the place is for sale. However, I was sent a couple of wines for *Quaff* and (although I've been able to find out nothing about the wine) thought this was delightful: fresh, clean, zingy with ripe tropical flavours and some grassy herbal characters.

 PRETTY GOOD

2007 Banrock Station Semillon Chardonnay $9

The Riverland is one of the big losers with the current troubles being caused by the drought but Constellation's Banrock Station continues to offer clean, fresh and uncomplicated whites that make for good drinking.

2008 De Bortoli 'Montage' Chardonnay Semillon $9.95

This is a Riverina white that has fresh sweet pea flavours and is clean and pleasant, if a bit too sweetish for me.

2007 De Bortoli 'Sacred Hill' Traminer Riesling $7.95

This is a good example of traminer riesling – aromatic with pleasant grapey flavours finishing clean and sweet. Too sweet for me but it will be popular, especially at the price.

2007 Peter Lehmann Semillon Chardonnay $13.50

This has been a reliable performer in *Quaff* and while it's not a riot of flavour (as plenty of the other Peter Lehmann wines are) it's fresh and clean with some depth – a pleasant quaffer.

2007 Water Wheel 'Memsie' Chardonnay Sauvignon Blanc $12
Bendigo's Water Wheel has the habit of turning up some incredible quaffing wines from time to time. This has ripe, sweet fruit, a pleasing juiciness and a sweetish finish.

2008 Yalumba 'Christobel's' Classic Dry White $14.95
This is fine and delicate with clean, fresh flavours and is decent current drinking.

Blushing beauties

Pink wines under $15

PINK WINES UNDER $15

The rosé revolution continues and, if anything, has gathered more force over the past two years. It has swept rosé to a prominence only dreamt of by a few visionaries until recently. Interestingly, the trend is international, with the significant British wine market taking to the pink drop with the same zeal as wine lovers in Australia.

Below $15, the majority of rosés have some residual sugar. This style is enormously popular. The challenge for me is to differentiate between those that have a small amount of residual sugar to flesh them out, smoothen the palate and to make them easier to drink, and those which have residual sugar to make them sweet. The latter often fail by being too sweet and cloying. If you prefer your rosés dry, as I do, you'll find some to please you in this chapter. I suspect that the number may be on the increase.

Like so many of the wines that are produced to be drunk early, screwcaps are now universal. I applaud the continued use of screwcaps with all the rosés received for this chapter. This means that vibrant youthful freshness will be part of your experience of drinking rosé.

THE QUAFF 2009 'Run for the Roses'
PINK WINE OF THE YEAR

On the shortlist for this award are:
2008 Angoves 'Nine Vines' Grenache Shiraz Rosé
2007 De Bortoli 'Windy Peak' Cabernet Rosé
2008 Scarpantoni 'Ceres' Rosé
2007 Yalumba 'Y Series' Sangiovese Rosé
I think that Angoves has found an approach to making rosé in the vineyard and winery that works admirably and both the 2007 and newly arrived 2008 are looking great. I also love the style of this 'Windy Peak' and its savoury dryness. Scarpantoni is back on track with a super rosé utilising the natural fruitiness of gamay, while everything that Yalumba seems to touch tastes marvellous, especially the 'Y Series'. There's a nice balance here of fruitiness, the hint of sweetness and yet a crisp, fine finish. There are some wonderful rosés around and those shortlisted make a marvellous group. However, the **2007 De Bortoli 'Windy Peak' Cabernet Rosé** goes with food admirably and is the dry style I most enjoy drinking. It's the *Quaff 2009* Pink Wine of the Year.

The reliables –
consistent-quality wines, year in, year out

Australia's pink wines have not proved to be all that consistent over the years. Perhaps they suffer a bit more in lesser vintages. Certainly some of our Barossa and McLaren favourites suffered in the 2007 drought. For example, the most consistent rosé of the previous three years, the Scarpantoni 'Ceres' Rosé, didn't come up brilliantly in our tasting last year. Fortunately, it's looking great in 2008. The Angoves 'Nine Vines' Grenache Shiraz Rose (trophy winner at the 2006 National Wine Show in Canberra), the Yalumba 'Y Series' Sangiovese and the Mt Hurtle have been the most consistent performers in this price range in the past couple of years.

Buying and Drinking Pink Wines – Some Tips

Fresh is best
I'm a great believer that rosés are best drunk young. A healthy majority (10 out of 15) of the recommended rosés in this year's *Quaff* are from the 2008 or 2007 harvests, which means that they will be wonderfully fresh. The Mt Hurtle is the exception that proves the rule.

Now that the revolution is here
While more rosés are more widely available in Australia than ever before, this is not the time for complacency. Support those winemakers who have been overwhelmed by the tide of public opinion and given us what we wanted. More choice: more rosés. Continue supporting the rosé push!

BLOODY GOOD

2007 Angoves 'Nine Vines' Grenache Shiraz Rosé $14.95

2008 Angoves 'Nine Vines' Grenache Shiraz Rosé $14.95

I reported last year that the 2006 was very fruity while young and developed more savoury character with bottle age. I wondered if this would happen with the 2007 vintage. Well, it did. As a youngster, it was soft, round and very easy to drink (thanks to the low 12.5% alcohol), and was ripe, plump and juicy with gentle dry acidity to cleanse the palate. When tasted in June this year, it was restrained and more savoury yet still clean, fresh and vibrant with a very attractive dry finish. It's a great Australian rosé style.

At the last minute, the 2008 'Nine Vines' arrived. It's bloody good! It's bright pink, clean and fresh with attractive gravelly, earthy savoury flavours, finishing crisp, zingy and quite dry.

2007 Celestial Bay 'Goose Chase' Rosé $14.95

Here's a new Margaret River producer making a rosé from malbec and shiraz. It's bright pink, has intense raspberry, redcurrant and strawberry flavours, is bright and lively with fresh cleansing acidity so that it finishes dry and long.

2007 De Bortoli 'Windy Peak' Cabernet Rosé $15.20
THE QUAFF 2009 'Run for the Roses'
PINK WINE OF THE YEAR
For those who enjoy a dry style of rosé, this Victorian light-bodied cabernet is just terrific. It's restrained, soft, round and delicious, neatly balanced, savoury, finishing long and dry.

2006 Mt Hurtle Grenache Rosé $8.95

I tasted this a couple of times last year, including for *Quaff 2008*, and I've seen it again for this year's guide. It was rated 'Bloody Good' then I think it's drinking even better now. Normally, I'd be suspicious about a rosé with some age: in this case, the suspicion is completely unfounded. The 2006 Mt Hurtle is still fresh and clean, gentle, delicate and restrained with intense savoury flavours that give a mid-palate tang before a nicely dry finish. Great value. Quaff on!

2007 Pfeiffer 'Ensemble' $13.90

And well may Chris Pfeiffer call this wine 'Ensemble' as it's a blend of cabernet, merlot, shiraz, cabernet franc, viognier and malbec. I'm wondering what's the world record for grape varieties in one wine. It's a very nice dark plummy red from a tough vintage at Rutherglen: bright, fresh and clean with full flavour of raspberries and dark cherries, balanced sweetness in the mid-palate before a crisply pleasing finish with a touch of sweetness. I notice that the Pfeiffer website suggests pairing this with sweet-corn fritters, a favourite of mine: inspired.

2008 Scarpantoni 'Ceres' Rosé $14

I was disappointed by the previous vintage of 'Ceres' after several years when the wine was outstanding, in fact, as good as it gets. Well, you'll be as delighted as I am that the Scarpantoni 'Ceres' is back on form. The McLaren Vale had a perfect 2008 vintage, at least until that heatwave. Naturally enough, all the rosé was well and truly picked before that happened. It's made from the Beaujolais variety, gamay, which suits the rosé style admirably. This is an attractive crimson colour, is fruity, vibrant, soft, round and juicy with ripe sweet fruit (strawberries, redcurrant pastille) and is neatly balanced so that there's a touch of sweetness to finish.

2007 Sevenhill 'Lost Boot' Rosé $13.95

From the Clare Valley's Jesuit winery comes this very attractive, spicy rosé that has ripe strawberry and red cherry flavours, is fine, delicate and neatly balanced before finishing clean, fresh and crisp.

2007 Wirra Wirra 'Mrs Wigley' Rosé $16.50

It's that wretched cat (Mrs Wigley) again. Last year, it was winemaker Sam Connew's chocolate labrador, Murphy Brown, groaning about a wine being named after a cat. This year, it's Fling (the noble, well-behaved, hungry beagle) who's woof, woofing (he hasn't quite learnt to bark) in protest. Lucky, it's a decent wine. There's some restraint and delightful balance, gravelly savoury characters, even complexity, before a crisp, clean, long, dryish finish.

2007 Yalumba 'Y Series' Sangiovese Rosé $12.95

This is a leap up on the 2007 and back to the quality of the 2006: it has ripe sweet redcurrant and red cherry flavours, a plumpness in the mid-palate, and a pleasant dryish finish that lingers.

 **GOOD**

2007 Barking Owl Rosé $17.95

This is the second label of Perth Hills winery Millbrook. The marketing guys say that it's often discounted below $15 so look for those buying opportunities. The wine itself is a pleasant, easy-drinking rosé with spicy, sweet ripe fruit – red cherry jube and blackberry pastille flavours – before a clean, dryish finish.

2008 De Bortoli 'Sacred Hill' Rose $7.50

The De Bortoli team often hits the mark with this bargain-basement brand – as they do with this delicious juicy, light-bodied rosé: bright red berry fruit and a clean zingy finish with a touch of sweetness.

2008 Kirrihill 'Companions' Garnacha Rosé $13.50

A Clare Valley grenache rosé (why Kirrihill used the Spanish term 'garnacha' I'm at a loss to understand) that is in the sweeter style: soft, round and easy to like, it has medium intensity, some redcurrant and pink musk flavours before a clean, crisp finish that shows a touch of sweetness.

2008 Pitchfork Pink $16

With outstanding winemaker Mike Kerrigan now involved as general manager and part-owner, Hay Shed Hill is moving forward. It shows, even in the humble Pitchfork Pink. It's made from cabernet and is supple, round and very approachable, with ripe strawberry and red cherry flavours and a crisp, clean, dry finish.

2007 Taltarni 'T Series' Rosé $14.95

A Central Victorian rosé that delivers exactly what you want: a wine that is light, bright and far too easy to drink. As well as that, there's some ripe redcurrant and red cherry flavours, balanced by a savouriness that leaves a pleasant, dryish aftertaste.

2007 Taylors 'Promised Land' White Cabernet Rosé $13.95

There's plenty to like in this floral Clare Valley rosé with overtones of ripe cherries and red plums: it's very soft and easy to drink and finishes crisp, clean and quite dry.

2008 Willow Bridge Rosé $15.50

From Geographe and the Ferguson Valley near Bunbury comes this crisp, clean, fruity rosé made from shiraz and cabernet. There's a hint of stalkiness but, for the most part, it is balanced, dry and crisp with a lingering spicy aftertaste that grips gently.

2007 Zonte's Footstep Rosé $14.95

> This is brightly, and deeply, vibrantly fruited – a riot of raspberry and redcurrant that is fresh, pristine and concentrated before a pleasingly dry finish.

▶ PRETTY GOOD

2007 Innocent Bystander 'Growers' Rosé $14.95

> This is a restrained rosé made from pinot noir that appears drier at first than it is. It's smooth, textural and interesting: a rosé for reflecting on rather than just gulping.

2007 Jacobs Creek 'Three Vines' Shiraz Grenache Sangiovese $14.95

> Here is the second vintage of a quaffing label from the team at Jacobs Creek. The blend combines the Barossa's two great strengths – shiraz and grenache – with the Tuscan variety sangiovese, which adds some savoury notes to the wine. It's fine, sweet and fruity with good intensity and a pleasant grip to finish.

2008 McPherson Cabernet Rosé $10.95

> This Nagambie Lakes winery has produced a pleasant redcurrant and red cherry–flavoured rosé that is nicely filled out on the mid-palate by sweetness, finishing clean, zingy and sweet.

2008 Oxford Landing Rosé $8.95

> This will appeal to many people: it's fragrant with ripe redcurrant, red cherry flavours and just a hint of confectionery, boiled lolly characters, but finishes fresh, clean, vibrant and sweet.

2008 Trentham Estate 'La Famiglia' Sangiovese Rosé $14

> This is an excellent example of the sweetish style that many consumers love. It has fragrant, lifted cherry aromas, is sweet with a slight confectionery taste on the mid-palate before finishing fresh, clean and sweet.

Barbecue wines

Red wines under $15

THE QUAFF 2009 'Wagyu Steak and Chips'
RED WINE OF THE YEAR AWARD

On the shortlist for this award are:
2004 Buller 'Beverford' Durif
2006 De Bortoli 'Deen Vat 1' Durif
2006 Elderton 'E' Shiraz Cabernet
2006 Kingston Estate Petit Verdot
2007 Sandalford 'Element' Cabernet Sauvignon
2006 Trentham Estate Pinot Noir
2007 Yalumba 'Galway Vintage' Shiraz

Anyone who is not convinced of the quality of Australian quaffing wines needs only to taste these reds. The Trentham Estate Pinot is an unlikely contender, but it shows what the Murphy boys at Mildura can do. Having access to plenty of fruit and taking advantage of what their area does best works well for Elderton with its Barossa red blend and for Sandalford and its Western Australia cabernet. In quality terms, there's little to separate the Buller and De Bortoli Durifs: they are both robust reds (as you'd expect) that can be drunk now with huge enjoyment. The Kingston Petit Verdot illustrates just how suitable this variety is to so many parts of Australia. But the **2007 Yalumba 'Galway Vintage' Shiraz** ... wines like this are the reason that *Quaff* exists. This is a classic Aussie shiraz that overdelivers on price. It is fragrant, deeply flavoured, beautifully textured, impeccably balanced: and a worthy winner of *Quaff*'s Red Wine of the Year.

THE QUAFF 2009 'Sausages and Chips'
BEST RED WINE UNDER $10 AWARD

On the shortlist for this award are:
2007 Angoves 'Long Row' Cabernet Sauvignon
2007 Banrock Station Shiraz Cabernet
2007 Oxford Landing Shiraz
2007 Queen Adelaide 'Regency Red' Shiraz Cabernet
2007 Talinga Park Cabernet Merlot
The Angoves, Banrock Station and Oxford Landing are excellent examples of quaffing reds from the Riverland – a region that knows how to do budget-priced reds in spite of the horrific drought. They are ripe, flavoursome wines, straightforward, but soft and silky in the mid-palate and gentle and balanced to finish. In terms of depth of flavour, Oxford Landing has the edge here. A former winner, the Talinga Park from the Riverina, is a strong contender. There's depth of flavour and a fragrant lift to the wine. The 'Regency Red' too is a former winner – five years ago in 2004, with its 2002 vintage. I'm amazed by the **2007 Queen Adelaide 'Regency Red' Shiraz Cabernet**, which has a slight edge with its fleshy texture, riotous flavours and delightful approachability. It's the *Quaff 2009* Best Red Wine under $10.

CABERNET SAUVIGNON

Cabernet sauvignon is certainly a much harder sell now than it used to be. The reality is that it is one of the classic wines of the world, does particularly well in many parts of Australia, and makes many brilliant wines – at all price points. That's why the best wines in this chapter are well worth considering. Producers have been forced to drop the price of their cabernets in order to get consumers interested in them. However, it's a well-worn *Quaff* notion that if something is unfashionable, it is likely to represent much better value than something that is trendy. So get on board with untrendy cabernet.

There appear to have been some improvements in the quality and approachability of cabernets under $15 over the past few years. In the past, I have found that cabernet's high levels of tannin (the drying grippiness you feel on the sides of your tongue and gums) made the wines sturdy, even confronting – especially when compared with more supple, fleshy and less firmly tannic varieties such as shiraz and grenache. There now appears more approachability and a lighter hand in the use of oak, which makes the wines easier to love – or, at least, more pleasant to cuddle.

The reliables –
consistent-quality wines, year in, year out

Still the nation's most consistent cabernet sauvignon at this price point is the popular Lindemans 'Bin 45', which has appeared in all but one edition of *Quaff* and remains good value.

Buying and Drinking Cabernet Sauvignon – Some Tips

Short-term cellaring
Most cabernets made at this price point are designed to be approachable so that they can be consumed young. As a general rule, if they are priced below $12 they won't drink any better than they will when you buy them. They should be drunk within six months or so – although they may last perfectly well for longer. If they are priced above $12, they may well benefit from short-term cellaring (six months to a year or two) as they are likely to mellow a bit and become an even better drink. If you are going to cellar some wine, store it in the coolest, darkest room you can find – ideally one without much temperature variation. You'll find that the better the storage conditions, the longer you can keep the wine.

Cabernet sauvignon and food
I generally drink wine with food. If I were to be drinking a red wine at a party or in some situation without food, I would avoid cabernet sauvignon. I'd be looking for something much gentler. With food, however, it's a different matter. Cabernet can be transformed by food. It appears much softer, more supple, even more mellow – those tannins appear to be gulped up by the food. Best matches include full-flavoured meat dishes – steak, roast lamb, venison or kangaroo fillets, especially served with robust red-wine sauces – and hard cheeses such as parmesan or cheddar. Appropriate matches can include casseroles such as lamb shanks, osso buco or coq au vin – especially if you can slip a bit of the wine into the dish.

▶ BLOODY GOOD

2007 Angoves 'Long Row' Cabernet Sauvignon $9.95

A Riverland cabernet that has plenty of oak and tannins but is balanced by the depth of dark berry fruit. There's some silky texture to round out the picture.

2005 Moondah Brook Cabernet Sauvignon $18

A Western Australian red in a great vintage in the state for cabernet. There's interesting and concentrated flavours – blackberry, coffee, chocolate characters – that go deep and long; texturally strong and seductively silky.

2007 Sandalford 'Element' Cabernet Sauvignon $14

One of the best reds I've seen under the entry level 'Element' range and another triumph for the team led by Paul Boulden. This is exactly what I was talking about in the introduction about winemakers looking to produce more approachable cabernet at this price point. It's soft, round, medium-bodied, juicy, with ripe raspberry and blackberry flavours that have just a hint of tobacco leaf. This is succulent, silky smooth and neatly balanced.

2007 Yalumba 'Y Series' Cabernet Sauvignon $12.95

Another excellent red from the Yalumba 'Y Series' range. It's soft, round and juicy, medium-bodied with rich black-currant flavours, a hint of leafiness and a supple, gentle finish.

▶ GOOD

2005 Long Flat 'Destinations' Cabernet Sauvignon $14.95

Cheviot Bridge's virtual winery has fashioned this cabernet from Coonawarra fruit in the very good 2005 vintage. There are brooding aromas, dense brambly, blackcurrant and dark chocolate flavours, smooth texture and substantial tannins to close. The winery's website recommends serving it with char-grilled rib eye steaks with creamy mushroom sauce and sweet potato mash. I'll go along with that.

2006 Scarpantoni 'Pedler Creek' Cabernet Sauvignon $14

> Just what you expect and want from McLaren Vale cabernet: supple, rich blackcurrant and dark plum flavours with vanilla-bean oak. Easy to like.

2007 Woop Woop Cabernet Sauvignon $13

> Here's Ben Riggs and Tony Parkinson (from Penny's Hill) making some good quaffing red from Langhorne Creek. There's blackberry pastille and ripe plummy fruit, smooth almost silky texture and attractive balance. Very drinkable.

2005 Wyndham Estate 'Bin 444' Cabernet Sauvignon $14.95

> I enjoyed this for its attractive texture, juicy succulence, and bright, ripe, sweet redcurrant pastille flavours.

2007 Zilzie Cabernet Sauvignon $14.95

> There's an attractive fragrance to the wine, soft, red cherry flavours, succulence in the mid-palate with a balanced finish that pleases.

▬ PRETTY GOOD

2006 High Country Cabernet Sauvignon $13.95

> This is the old Miranda label now owned by Icon Brands. There plenty of vanilla bean, dense blackberry flavours, smooth texture and substantial tannins. For those who like the style.

2005 Kingston Estate Cabernet Sauvignon $12.95

> An easy-drinking cabernet that has ripe plummy flavours, smooth texture and approachable tannins.

2007 Lindemans 'Bin 45' Cabernet Sauvignon $10.95

> One of the Reliables and so consistently rated in *Quaff.* This vintage is supple, round and silky smooth with dense, powerful, rich and concentrated dark berry flavours. Just a tad oaky.

2006 McGuigan Cabernet Sauvignon $12.95

There's drinkability here, smooth dark berry flavours and a pleasing mid-palate softness. However, a bit firm to finish.

2007 McPherson Cabernet Sauvignon $10.95

This is pretty oaky with substantial tannins and has dark berry, chocolate and vanilla-bean character so there's reasonable balance.

2007 Penfolds 'Rawsons Retreat' Cabernet Sauvignon $11.95

There's some red cherry, redcurrant jubes and sarsaparilla flavours in this soft, easy-drinking wine.

2007 Saltram 'Maker's Table' Cabernet Sauvignon $10.95

There's heaps of oak, tannin and fruit – plenty of dark berry, vanilla-bean and liquorice characters – and reasonable balance.

2007 Thorn Clarke 'Sandpiper' Cabernet Sauvignon $14.95

This is a robust, full-on red that has dense liquorice and cassis flavours and big tannins.

2006 Vintage Cellars Cabernet Sauvignon $13.95

There is strong coconutty oak, restrained herbal characters: many will like the oaky style. Exclusive to Vintage Cellars.

2004 Western Range 'Old Well' Cabernet Sauvignon $9

From the Perth Hills winery, based in the Chittering Valley, here is a soft, round cabernet that has little concentration but is a pleasant drink.

MERLOT

There's plenty of merlot grown these days. Red wine production in Australia dropped by about 35% in the difficult 2007 vintage, but bounced back almost to 2006 figures the following year. The amount of merlot produced has increased by more than 30%, from 93,000 tonnes in 2003 to 129,000 tonnes in 2008 (when the intake of shiraz was 436,000 tonnes and cabernet 254,000 tonnes). Putting it in historical perspective, the rise and rise of merlot is phenomenal: only 1000 tonnes were produced Australia-wide in 1988 and 8000 tonnes in 1996.

Merlot is much loved and much maligned. At its rare best – when it is ripe, silkily textured, in harmony with gentle oak – it can be immediately appealing and a great drink. As a varietal in Australia, too often it is thin, green, weedy, over-oaked and completely lacking in charm. Those who see wines like the latter can have some sympathy with Miles, in the film *Sideways*, and his comment, 'I'm leaving if anyone orders merlot.' My household is dominated by one person who likes merlot a lot more than me.

While plenty of expensive merlots disappoint, there are many very drinkable merlots at the quaffing price point. In fact, it seems that when the winemakers chill out and don't try too hard – by cramming too much oak into the wine or extracting every last ounce of tannin – the result can be much more drinkable, a fun-filled, juicy red fruit bomb that is a pleasure to gulp. Don't doubt it for a second: merlot is still popular, especially in *Quaff*land.

The reliables –
consistent-quality wines, year in, year out

The McWilliams 'Hanwood' has appeared in all but one edition of *Quaff*, making it the most consistent and reliable example of the variety at the price.

Buying and Drinking Merlot – Some Tips

Balance is all

You'll see very clearly the style of merlot that I believe makes the best drink: wines that don't have too much oak or tannin, which are not over-extractive, and those that aren't too heavy or too strong. This means that the wines need to be balanced – the fruit should match the oak treatment and the tannins. As a general rule, wines at this price point have neither the richness nor concentration to cope with a great deal of oak or massive tannins. That's why merlot is often at its best when it's least manipulated.

Different styles

Having stated a clear preference for soft, smooth, easy-drinking and fleshy merlots (especially at the *Quaff* price point), it should be said that I also admire the bigger, bolder, more robust and savoury reds, which might finish dry and tannic: wines such as the powerful Thorn Clarke 'Sandpiper' Merlot and Capel Vale's 'Debut' from Geographe. These are different in style but avoid excessive oaking and heavy tannins.

▶ BLOODY GOOD

2007 Jacobs Creek Merlot $10.95

> A surprisingly good effort in a difficult year for many
> Australian wineries, this is supple, round and fleshy, has
> attractive rich plummy fruit, all neatly in balance with the
> oak and tannins. There's a slight grip to remind you this is
> red wine. A ravoli dish in a bolognaise ragu would suit
> admirably.

2005 Lindemans 'Reserve' Merlot $13.95

> This Limestone Coast varietal is an excellent example of
> quaffing merlot: it's soft, round and very easy to drink,
> with ripe, sweet blackberry and dark plum flavours, fleshy
> texture and substantial though balanced tannins, so it's
> nicely approachable.

2006 Thorn Clarke 'Sandpiper' Merlot $14.95

> Densely flavoured with deep, dark berry flavours, some
> chocolate and a fair whack of vanilla-bean oak. It's fleshy,
> moving towards velvety, and is very appealing.

2007 Wyndham Estate 'Bin 999' Merlot $14.95

> This is the kind of red that gives merlot respectability: it's
> deep, densely flavoured with ripe plum and blackberry,
> has a silky smooth texture and fine, persistent, slinky
> tannins. Try it with an elegant veal scaloppine with a red-
> wine sauce.

2007 Yalumba 'Y Series' Merlot $12.95

> Another pearl in Yalumba's brilliant value-for-money
> range. It is rich, ripe and concentrated with blackcurrant
> and black cherry flavours, fleshy, silky texture, and
> substantial, ripe, fine-knit tannins. Drink with an elegant
> lamb roast dish or the best new season's lamb chops.

▰▶ GOOD

2007 Capel Vale 'Debut' Merlot $16.95

The previous vintage was sensational and this appears to be following in its footsteps. I'm not certain it'll attain the same heights but it's early days now and the wine may develop further. It's soft, round and richly concentrated with dark plummy flavours, good weight and plenty of tannins.

2006 Hardys 'Nottage Hill' Merlot $10.50

Another of a good crop of reds from Constellation's Nottage Hill team. This is soft, round and smooth with ripe, sweet fruit and good balance. Impressive, and a bargain.

2007 Little Penguin Merlot $10.95

I've responded well before to the Little Penguin Merlot and find that I've scored it well again. It's soft, round and very smooth, fleshily textured, with plenty of oak and substantial tannins yet, for me at least, the fruit has the depth and weight to match that. I'd still look for a good Provençale beef stew.

2006 Logan 'Apple Tree Flat' Merlot $11

There's heaps of dense, ripe sweet plummy fruit, smooth and fleshy texture, good balance and plenty of fine, tight-knit tannins. A hearty t-bone steak and chips might be just the dish to accompany this.

2007 Penfolds 'Rawsons Retreat' Merlot $11.95

This is a delight from the Penfolds team: juicy redcurrant and red cherry flavours, pleasing succulence, smooth texture, balanced easy drinking.

2007 Sandalford 'Element' Merlot $14

Here's a pleasant surprise from Sandalford's entry-level range. Mind you, 2007 was a much better year in the West than it was in most other places. This is deep, dense and richly concentrated with ripe plummy flavours, smooth texture and admirable balance.

▆▶ PRETTY GOOD

2007 Angoves 'Long Row' Merlot $9.95

There are plenty of rich, concentrated plummy flavours but a dominant oaky edge gives it a firm finish. Try and tame it with a robust beef stew.

2006 Logan 'Weemala' Merlot $15.95

Merlot does well in Orange and so it's no surprise that this is a pleasant, flavoursome and approachable red with plummy flavour. For me, it's just a bit too firm to finish.

2006 Poet's Corner Merlot $9.95

Here is an easy-drinking merlot with pleasing dark berry flavours and noticeable tannins. Bring on the bangers and mash.

2007 Queen Adelaide Merlot $8.95

A light- to medium-bodied merlot that has smooth texture with a hint of fleshiness and ripe blackberry flavours.

2007 Redbank 'Long Paddock' Merlot $13.95

The Hill Smith family's King Valley label Redbank gives us a soft, round and easy-drinking merlot highlighting red cherry and plum flavours.

2006 Rosemount Estate 'Diamond Label' Merlot $15.95

Here is an easy-drinking merlot that has good depth, a savoury rather than fruity flavour profile, and so is a natural with food. I'm thinking of classy pork sausages and a rich gravy.

2007 Wolf Blass 'Eaglehawk' Merlot $9.95

This is light- to medium-bodied, with ripe, sweet red berry flavours, pleasingly juicy and a little grippy on the finish.

SHIRAZ

The hardy, vigorous shiraz grape has been an important part of Australia's viticultural history and has done well in our warm regions since the middle of the nineteenth century. It has been used to produce good-quality, fairly priced table wine; as fodder for cask and flagon wines; in cheap red blends (especially with grenache, cabernet sauvignon and mataro); and as a base wine for sparkling reds. With grenache, it has been an important source of fortified wine. However, in the 1980s shiraz was so unfashionable that the South Australian government offered incentives to grape growers to uproot their vines. Many now-priceless old vines were lost to the Vine Pull Scheme of 1985.

Today, shiraz is Australia's most popular red grape variety – with 436,000 tonnes harvested in 2007, exceeded only by chardonnay (444,000 tonnes) and ahead of its only red rival, cabernet sauvignon (260,000 tonnes). Shiraz had been well ahead of chardonnay until 2007 when the drought led to a reduction in yield of 35%. Although it bounced back in 2008 by 53% more than the previous year, it has still not overtaken chardonnay.

Plantings of shiraz increased sixfold in the 1990s and have further increased by 50% since 2003. While this huge increase in production has benefited our export drive and has kept down the price of quaffing wines, the most recent surge has resulted in wines being made from an unprecedented number of young vines. These can taste thin, lean and lacking in fruit; winemakers may attempt to disguise this with excessive oak flavour (by throwing too many coarse-tasting oak chips into the fermentation vats), or by adding too much tannin or leaving in too much residual sugar. The resulting wines are out of balance and taste awful. You have been saved from trying them.

There's no question about Aussie shiraz making great quaffing reds. Throughout the country, wineries are able to produce attractive, delightfully flavoursome shiraz with excellent texture and approach-ability. Most importantly, they are well priced. Especially at the moment, when many Australian quaffing wines are a dollar or more cheaper than at this time last year – or in some cases, five years ago. The best wines can come from such diverse regions as the Barossa, McLaren Vale, Padthaway, Mudgee, Frankland River, Heathcote and the Adelaide Hills.

Buying and Drinking Shiraz – Some Tips

Drink now

If you are looking for a spicy red that is light- to medium-bodied, soft and approachable, you'll find some excellent examples under $12. These invariably come from the Riverina, Murray–Darling, Swan Hill or Riverland, and can be great wines for immediate drinking.

Cellaring

More substantial, more full-bodied shiraz tends to be in the $12 to $15 range and usually contains a proportion of fruit from premium areas such as Coonawarra, Clare, Langhorne Creek or McLaren Vale, or are sourced entirely from one of these regions. These can be drunk now but need to be served with robust or hearty meat dishes, to soften the impact of powerful tannins. They should repay even short-term cellaring (and the better your cellaring conditions, the longer you can keep the wines).

▭ BLOODY GOOD

2006 De Bortoli 'Windy Peak' Shiraz Viognier $15.95

Another very good quaffer under the 'Windy Peak' label. It's soft, round and smooth, with dark berry flavours that are well integrated with the oak, almost velvety texture, finishing with a firm grip. Needs a satisfying slow-cooked Italian dish like osso buco to bring out its best.

2006 Hardys 'Nottage Hill' Shiraz $10.50

It's increasingly hard to find 'Bloody Good' shiraz at close to $10 so that makes it worth your while to look at this silky smooth, richly concentrated red with ripe blackberry flavours and warm coconutty oak.

2007 Oxford Landing Shiraz $8.95

This is made by the team at Yalumba so they've had a very good year. This is medium bodied with ripe, deep blackberry and plum flavours, very soft and smooth in the mid-palate with a clean, fresh finish. You can't ask for more at the price.

2005 Vintage Cellars Shiraz $13.95

This is my favourite of the wines under the Vintage Cellars own label: there's heaps of coconutty oak, rich concentrated mocca, coffee, chocolate and plum flavours, silky smooth texture and pleasing approachability. Exclusive to Vintage Cellars.

2006 Westend 'Calabria' Shiraz Viognier $14.95

Bill Calabria's family has been running Westend since 1945 so it's fair enough that there should be the occasional wine that celebrates that achievement. There are some attractive floral aromas, delicate redcurrant pastille flavours, light to medium body, silky smooth texture and balanced acidity and tannins to finish. Good quaffing.

2007 Willow Bridge Shiraz $15.50

A fine Western Australian producer which makes very good shiraz. This is its entry-level red and is fabulous at the price. It's soft, round and vibrant with juicy, sweet redcurrant and dark plum flavours, power and drive. Approachable now and very satisfying.

2007 Yalumba 'Galway Vintage' Shiraz $14.95

THE 2009 OBERON KANT MEMORIAL AWARD FOR
THE QUINTESSENTIAL QUAFFER,
THE ULTIMATE AUSTRALIAN WINE UNDER $15 and
THE QUAFF 2009 'Wagyu Steak and Chips'
RED WINE OF THE YEAR AWARD

These three Yalumba Shiraz are a revelation and this was my preferred wine, by a whisker. There are lifted spicy aromas, ripe blackberry pastille and dark plum flavours that are rich and wonderfully concentrated, finishing fine and balanced with a gentle grip. It's fresh and beautifully clean with a touch of class.

2007 Yalumba 'Y Series' Shiraz $12.95

Unlike the previous two vintages, I liked this a fraction more than the Shiraz Viognier. Its texture is extraordinary, gently velvety in the mid-palate. The dark berry characters are deep and long and the tannins are ripe, fine-knit and approachable. It's drinking well now.

2007 Yalumba 'Y Series' Shiraz Viognier $12.95

This is a terrific quaffing red – soft, round and very easy to drink: rich, dark cherry and plum flavours, and gentle, supple tannins.

GOOD

2007 Angoves 'Red Belly Black' Shiraz $14.95

There's generosity here, an almost lush easy-drinking quality as rich, concentrated plummy flavours are presented in an approachable style.

2004 Growers 'Peppermint Grove' Shiraz Viognier $14.95

> Here is a Western Australian shiraz that is soft and juicy, has reasonable depth of flavour and length, smooth texture and a good aftertaste.

2006 Kingston Estate Shiraz $12.95

> This is a vibrant medium-bodied Riverland shiraz that has decent plummy fruit and drinks well now.

2006 Kirrihill 'Companions' Shiraz Viognier $14.95

> I rated this blend of Clare and Adelaide Hills shiraz 'Good' in last year's *Quaff* and have tasted it twice since. Most recently, I thought its coconutty, vanilla-bean oak now appeared less dominant and, although there's plenty of oak still, it is better integrated. There's ripe, sweet dark berry fruit, silky smooth texture. If you like the style, it's drinking well.

2006 Logan 'Weemala' Shiraz Viognier $15.95

> There are some beguiling white pepper characters on the nose, then redcurrant and dark plum flavours and pleasing fleshiness. It's a wine that I enjoyed but others in the panel were less enthusiastic, feeling that it might be a bit underripe. If you like that white pepper character, I think you'll be delighted – but it may divide opinion.

2005 Taminick Cellars '1919 Series' Shiraz $14

> Like Ned Kelly, this Taminick's of Glenrowan Shiraz may split public opinion. It's unusual but seductive. There are lashings of rich, ripe caramel chocolate flavours, lush almost syrupy texture, richness, concentration and moderate tannins.

2007 Thorn Clarke 'Sandpiper' Shiraz $14.95

> There are heaps of juicy, vibrant satsuma plum flavours in this Barossa shiraz. It's delicately balanced with plenty of oak and tannins.

2006 Tobacco Road Shiraz $13

Here is another label of the Alpine Valleys winery. It's a soft, smooth and easy-drinking style that is ripe, rich and reasonably concentrated.

2005 Tyrrells 'Midnight Leap' Shiraz $10.95

There's heaps of ripe, rich, sweet strawberry, raspberry and red cherry flavours, smooth texture and supple, approachable finish.

2006 Xanadu 'Dragon' Shiraz $16

The glory days are back at Xanadu under Rathbone ownership, with a focus clearly on producing quality Margaret River wines. Here winemaker Glenn Goddall combines soft, fleshy texture with rich, plum and white pepper flavours and easy-drinking approachability.

➤ PRETTY GOOD

2006 Angoves 'Long Row' Shiraz $9.95

Decent easy-drinking shiraz with dark plum, redcurrant and tomato bush flavours.

2007 Angoves 'Nine Vines' Shiraz Viognier $14

There are concentrated dark plum characters here and decent smooth texture but the tannins dominate the finish and it's a bit grippy. Perhaps the barbecue is the perfect scenario to enjoy this.

2005 Barking Owl Shiraz Viognier $16.95

This is the second label for Perth Hills–based Millbrook and is sourced widely from around Western Australia. It's an approachable shiraz that is fresh, clean and bright, medium-bodied, smoothly textured with redcurrant and plum flavours.

2006 Cookoothama Shiraz $14.95

> Now this wine will divide opinion. Some will love its bold vanilla-bean characters and robust oaky style. Others will find it over the top. You decide.

2006 Hardys 'Shuttles' Shiraz (187 ml) $5

> Rich dark berry and brambly flavours and chewy tannins.

2007 Lindemans 'Bin 50' Shiraz $10.95

> There are good dark berry flavours, smooth texture and quite dominant coconutty oak.

2006 Lindemans 'Reserve' Shiraz $13.95

> This has redcurrant and dark plum flavours, is soft and round in the mid-palate, and finishes with vanillin characters and some coconutty oak.

2006 Long Flat 'Destinations' Shiraz $14.95

> This Barossa shiraz has deep dark berry flavours with plenty of oak.

2007 McPherson Shiraz $10.95

> This is supple, clean and round, with fresh redcurrant and plum flavours and approachable tannins.

2006 Plantagenet 'Hazard Hill' Shiraz $12

> The entry-level Plantagenet shiraz shows some of the effects of the difficult 2006 vintage for reds in the West, especially in its firm finish. In spite of that there is some pleasant softness on the mid-palate and good flavours.

2006 Rock Paper Scissors Shiraz Viognier $9.95

> There's richness and concentrated flavours and fresh chewy tannins.

2007 Xabregas Shiraz $14.95

A well-priced shiraz from Mt Barker (in the West), from a newish producer who sells fruit to some of the established large companies: this has vibrant redcurrant, raspberry and plum flavours, smooth texture, and is a little firm to finish.

OTHER RED VARIETALS

I was tasting my way through most of the other red varietals, seeing the occasional very good wine and a few that failed to excite, when I hit the final bracket. Because there are so many different varieties in the tasting I didn't have a clue what was coming up (usually you have know what varieties you are tasting). All of a sudden, I'm wondering what we were tasting because there was red wine after red wine that was just superb. It was as though we were tasting wines that were much more expensive than quaffing reds. It turned out that it was a bracket of durif, petit verdot and malbec. You'll see them in the 'Bloody Good' section. Be warned, these are terrific quaffing wines.

The wines in this chapter include grape varieties that have been around in Australia for some time – malbec, pinot noir, petit verdot durif, as well as tarrango – and some classic European varieties that are beginning to be planted in significant amounts – sangiovese, tempranillo and nebbiolo. It's a pretty diverse bunch.

There is heaps of excitement with the best of these wines. Many provide taste experiences outside the mainstream and are recommended for much the same reason as I'd advocate trying some exotic varieties that have been imported from overseas: being adventurous can be fun.

The reliables –
consistent-quality wines, year in, year out

The wonderfully robust Bleasdale Malbec is one of the Reliables and has been included in every edition of *Quaff*. The 2005 is as good as I've ever seen it. Labels that have consistently appeared in this chapter include De Bortoli 'Windy Peak' (replaced by 'Deen' this year), Trentham Estate and Zilzie.

Buying and Drinking Other Red Varietals – Some Tips

Drink unfashionably

I may have mentioned in passing that the best value you'll find will be with wines that are unfashionable. Here is the perfect example: durif, petit verdot and malbec all make great varietal reds, which at their best are full-bodied, full-flavoured, sumptuous and beautifully textured. But they are hard to sell.

Get together with some friends over a dinner party, cook up some robust, slow-cooked dishes and try the malbec, two of the durif and two of the petit verdot from the 'Bloody Good' section. Or do it as a tasting. You'll be blown away.

The perfect match

Thinking about what wines will go best with what foods should probably start with traditional matches. Duck and pinot noir are considered a classic pairing, although I believe that lighter bodied meats such as veal and pork will also work well – especially when the dish incorporates mushrooms, which find an earthy echo in the wine. Sangiovese goes well with many Tuscan dishes, and also try roast pork, tomato-based pasta dishes, or even pizza. More full-bodied reds such as malbec, durif and petit verdot demand robust, slow-cooked meat dishes or grilled steak with hearty red-wine sauces.

BLOODY GOOD

2005 Bleasdale Malbec $14.95

This is the best Bleasdale Malbec that I can remember and, as one of our Reliables, it has always been consistently good. It has the depth of flavour and the lushness that I associate with Langhorne Creek. As well as that, it's dense with rich blackberry, dark plum, chocolate and vanilla-bean flavours, has smooth almost silky texture and a powerful, lingering finish.

2004 Buller 'Beverford' Durif $12

This is the best red I've seen from the Buller's Swan Hill vineyards under the Beverford label. It's supple, round and juicy with deeply concentrated rich and ripe dark berry flavours and its substantial tannins are balanced by fruit density and weight. Succulent, vibrant and with extra-good length.

2006 Coldstone Tempranillo $12

From the Victorian Alps Winery comes this appropriately named label and a tempranillo that drinks beautifully. There are rich, concentrated dark berry flavours, a smooth texture and substantial though non-aggressive tannins.

2006 De Bortoli 'Deen Vat 1' Durif $11.95

I suspect that durif may be a variety where cheaper is better. I wonder if some of the more expensive durifs are given too lavish treatment with oak which exaggerates their natural powerful tannins. There's a softness or an approachability about the durif I'm seeing here that I find particularly appealing. This is lushly concentrated, ripe, dense and powerful with bright dark berry flavours, a mouthfilling succulence and substantial yet balanced tannins. It's a robust red with a touch of elegance.

2006 De Bortoli 'Deen Vat 4' Petit Verdot $12.95

This makes a pair of outstanding varietal Deens for De Bortoli. The Vat 4 Petit Verdot has picked up a couple of gold medals (no surprise there) and is a lovely mix of ripe, sweet fruit and savoury dry tannins, of succulent, refreshing flavour and dense, full fruitiness. There's juicy dark berries, substantial tannins on an approachable dry finish that lingers.

2006 Kingston Estate Petit Verdot $12.95

Bill Moularadellis has been a big promoter of the variety and has planted heaps of it at Kingston-on-Murray in the Riverland. This is sourced from there, Langhorne Creek and the Murray–Darling and is a tremendous full-throttle example of petit verdot at its best: ripe, opulent, deeply concentrated with blackcurrant and mulberry flavours, lavish but balanced oak, lushly textured with substantial fine-knit tannins that are matched by the weight of the fruit. It is vibrant, juicy, powerful and approachable (one of the panel said 'friendly'). I'll drink to that. Quaff on!

2006 Trentham Estate Pinot Noir $12.50

This is a revelation because I don't expect pinot from Mildura to taste this good. It is medium-bodied, has richness of concentrated red cherry flavours, silky smooth texture, good weight and power, and soft, fine tannins. It has varietal character and is quite delicious.

2007 Wyndham Estate 'Bin 333' Pinot Noir $14.95

These two pinots make a good pair. Certainly it's rare to find two very pleasant drinking pinots with good varietal character for less than $15. This has attractive, ripe, sweet redcurrant and dark cherry flavours that gently persist. There's even a hint of complexity to add an interesting dimension.

2007 Zilzie Sangiovese $14.95

Good sangioveses are rare in Australia and rarer still at this price. This is clean and fresh, even vibrant, pleasantly juicy with fine savoury flavours and powerful tannins that are matched by fruit weight. Gnocchi and a tomato-based veal ragu sounds an interesting match.

▄▃ GOOD

2006 Casella 'Yendah' Sangiovese $15.95

There have been some terrific Italian varietals under this label from Casella, now beautifully packaged. There's plenty of oak and tannins but these are balanced by the powerful, dense blackberry, sour black cherry flavours before a pleasantly grippy finish. Try it with roast leg of lamb, trimmings and a robust wine sauce.

2005 Vintage Cellars Tempranillo $11.95

This powerful, robust red has been sourced from Heathcote and shows dense dark berry flavours with some vanilla bean and a hint of stalk. There are substantial fine-grained tannins on a pleasantly dry finish. Exclusive to Vintage Cellars.

2007 Westend 'Calabria' St Macaire $14.95

I guess if you had only 2 hectares of a French grape variety planted in Australia you'd want to flaunt it. In Bill Calabria's case his plantings are 30 years old, low-yielding for the area, and so he gets good concentration from the wine. St Macaire is a village on the opposite side of the river from Sauternes in Bordeaux so I would expect that to be the variety's likely origin. In 2007 the 'Calabria' St Macaire is deeply flavoured with ripe, sweet blackberry and dark plum flavours, is powerful, robust and smoothly textured. Approachable now.

⬤▶ PRETTY GOOD

2007 Brown Brothers Tarrango $12.90

This is a hybrid variety specially developed by the CSIRO to suit Australia's warm dry climate and it's a huge seller for Brown Brothers because of its appealing style. In 2007 it is light-bodied soft, round, has decent red berry flavours and is very easy to drink because of its mild tannins.

2007 Yering Station 'Mr Frog' Pinot Noir $14.95

This entry-level Yarra pinot noir has decent red berry flavours, restrained oak and gentle, smooth texture before a soft, gentle finish.

CABERNET MERLOT BLENDS

There have been huge amounts of merlot planted in the last decade in Australia and so there are many more varietal merlots and a plethora of cabernet merlot blends stocking the shelves in retail land. The ease of pronunciation and the sweet sound of the word 'merlot' have surely helped its popularity, as has its perceived softness.

The marriage of cabernet sauvignon, with its firmer structure, occasionally hollow mid-palate and drying grip, and merlot, with its fleshy smoothness, plump mid-palate and softer, gentler finish, can produce some beautifully balanced, flavoursome reds. But the reality is that only five out of more than 47 cabernet merlots I tasted have been rated 'Bloody Good'. Less than half of those tasted are reviewed in this section. Many of the other wines were either too powerful, oaky and almost unapproachable, or skinny and tough.

The reliables –
consistent-quality wines, year in, year out

This is an emerging category with no clear-cut Reliables over the nine years that *Quaff* has been coming out, but the most consistent in recent times has been De Bortoli.

Buying and Drinking Cabernet Merlot Blends – Some Tips

The $12 price point

There tends to be a division between those wines under $12 and those which sell for between $12 and $15. The best of the former have more redcurrant, raspberry flavours while the latter tend to have darker berry fruit – often because of the addition of up to 20% of fruit from some of Australia's premium regions. Those under $12 usually come from regions along the Murray River (the Riverland, Swan Hill and Murray–Darling) and the Murrumbidgee (the Riverina). They are lighter-bodied and more straightforward, but the best of them are delicious, everyday quaffers.

Bottle age

A number of the cabernet merlots that have been recommended come from premium regions and have enough richness and concentration of flavour and sufficient tannin grip to improve with time in your cellar. Grant Burge 'Barossa Vines' and Maxwell's 'Little Demon' are the wines most likely to benefit from additional bottle age. Having said that, the great thing about under-$15 wines is that they are approachable enough to drink now without having to worry about cellaring.

⬤▶ BLOODY GOOD

2006 De Bortoli 'Sero' Cabernet Merlot $14.20

This King Valley wine from De Bortoli has benefited from time in the bottle. It's softened and is now softer, rounder and fleshier than before – in fact, my tasting notes included the comment 'almost lush' and noted its good finish.

2006 Grant Burge 'Barossa Vines' Cabernet Merlot $16.30

On special, this will be a tempting Barossa red blend as it has a touch of elegance, very attractive ripe, sweet dark berry flavours, fleshy texture, tight structure and classy oak. There's some finesse, too, and the potential to age.

2005 Hardys 'Nottage Hill' Cabernet Merlot $10.50

Another notch on the belt for the team from Constellation. This is silky smooth, even fleshy, with blackcurrant and dark plum flavours, balanced fine, ripe tannins and an attractive finish.

2007 Talinga Park Cabernet Merlot $9.95

A favourite of mine, Best Red under $10 two years ago, and back in form. There are fragrant redcurrant pastille aromas, ripe, juicy red jubes and a hint of blackcurrant. Surprisingly concentrated considering its price, with some finesse before an attractive, balanced finish.

2007 Yellow Tail Cabernet Merlot $9.95

Australia's best-ever performer on the international stage is made by the Casella family in Griffith and it's now readily available in Australia. This is soft, round and fleshy with ripe, deep concentrated flavours, and balanced tannins. Drinking well.

GOOD

2005 Cockatoo Ridge Cabernet Merlot $9.95

This gets the entry-level Aussie cab merlot just right. It's soft, round and easy drinking, with ripe blackcurrant, fleshy texture and decent balance.

2007 De Bortoli 'Windy Peak' Cabernet Merlot $15.20

There's plenty of richness and concentration of deep blackcurrant and plum flavours, silky smooth texture. It is a bit firm to finish but it'll be fine if served with spaghettini and a ragu bolognaise.

2006 Penfolds 'Koonunga Hill' Cabernet Merlot $15.95

We've come to expect plenty of Koonunga Hill and here it delivers: rich, concentrated red berry flavours, very smooth texture and excellent balance. Good drinking.

2005 Vintage Cellars Cabernet Merlot $13.95

This is made for Vintage Cellars by one of the large players in the Great Southern. I think its use of American oak will split opinion about the wine: there's some warm vanilla bean, almost coconutty character. There's plenty of fruit but lots of oak too. If you like the style, this is for you. Exclusive to Vintage Cellars.

PRETTY GOOD

2007 Banrock Station Cabernet Merlot $9

There's good depth of flavour, plenty of oak and substantial tannins.

2007 De Bortoli 'Montage' Cabernet Merlot $9.95

Decent easy-drinking style that has pretty good dark berry flavours and smooth texture.

2006 McGuigan 'Black Label' Cabernet Merlot $9.95
> There's attractive fragrance, lively redcurrant and black cherry flavours and some succulence – pleasant quaffing.

2006 Maxwell 'Little Demon' Cabernet Merlot $16.95
> An entry-level McLaren Vale red blend from Mark Maxwell and the team that will appeal to those who love powerful coconutty American oak, dense, weighty fruit flavours and heaps of tannin. Demands a robust beef stew.

2006 Tyrrells 'Old Winery' Cabernet Merlot $13.95
> There's a pleasing richness and concentration, softness in the mid-palate, then slightly firm to finish.

2005 Wyndham Estate 'Bin 888' Cabernet Merlot $14.95
> A robust style that has deep blackcurrant and dark cherry flavours, some silky texture and substantial tannins. Drink with a hearty beef stew.

2006 Xanadu 'Dragon' Cabernet Merlot $16
> A pleasant, approachable red from a tricky vintage. It's soft and ripe and full flavoured, just a bit firm to finish.

GRENACHE BLENDS

Grenache has been one of Australia's most significant grape varieties because of its suitability for making fortifieds – until the last 30 years the most important style of wine produced here. Following the decline in the popularity of fortifieds since the 1970s, grenache was blended away into bulk and cask wines. Yet, as recently as the early 1990s, there was more grenache grown in Australia than cabernet sauvignon. Now there is about 12 times as much cabernet as grenache.

What has saved grenache has been the renewed interest in low-yielding, dry-grown old-vine grenache in regions such as the Barossa and McLaren Vale and the production of premium, super-premium or ultra-premium grenache from these vineyards. The opulent, power-fully concentrated, ripe, fleshy reds have sold for high prices and helped to forge reputations for the likes of Charles Melton, Torbreck, Turkey Flat, Kaesler, Hewitson, Clarendon Hills, D'Arenberg and newcomers such as Kilikanoon, Teusner and Kalleske.

There are a small number of deliciously vibrant quaffers – gener-ally grenache blends – that are appealing, gluggable, early-drinking reds at affordable prices. The 2007 Peter Lehmann Shiraz Grenache fits this category. The rest of the wines in this chapter are decent everyday reds. I suspect that most of the deliciously vibrant quaffers have become more expensive such as Hewitson's 'Miss Harry' (see the Great-Value Wines over $15 chapter, page 193).

The McLaren Vale are marketing grenache as Cadenzia and promoting it as one of the strengths of the region. Terrific wines, but closer to $25 in price.

The dearth of good grenache at the *Quaff* price point can also be attributed to the success of grenache as a blending component in rosés – and the enormous popularity of rosés.

The reliables –
consistent-quality wines, year in, year out
There's been a Peter Lehmann red ever-present in *Quaff*. What was originally marketed as a varietal grenache is now the Shiraz Grenache, while Lehmann added a Grenache Shiraz Mourvedre blend to the list from the 2003 vintage. D'Arenberg 'The Stump Jump' has been in seven out of the eight editions of *Quaff*.

Buying and Drinking Grenache Blends –
Some Tips

A blended red
Once again, no varietal grenaches have been featured in this chapter – just grenache blended with other reds that have an affinity with it. In its homeland, Spain, and in the south of France where it flourishes, grenache (garnacha in Spain) is most often used as part of a red blend.

Young, warm and wonderful
While there are a few exceptions – and they are not at this price point – grenache blends produced in Australia are best consumed young, when they are fresh, fleshy and flavoursome. They are so drinkable that there is no point in cellaring them.

🍾 GOOD

2007 Peter Lehmann Shiraz Grenache $13.50

There's heaps of ripe, sweet Barossa fruit, redcurrant and blackberry flavours, smooth, fleshy texture, and substantial tannins. A classy red that would be terrific with a roast leg of lamb, with all the trimmings.

🍾 PRETTY GOOD

2006 D'Arenberg 'The Stump Jump' Grenache Shiraz Mourvedre $11.95

This McLaren Vale red blend – also reviewed last year – is still looking pretty good. There's freshness of redcurrant and dark plum flavours still, good depth, and a gentle, grippy finish. Straightforward, easy drinking.

2007 Jacobs Creek Grenache Shiraz $10.95

There's plenty to like about this entry-level Jacobs Creek red: its ripe, sweet dark berry fruit with complexing earthiness, smooth texture and supple, balanced tannins. Better with food, such as with the best-quality sausages and mash or spaghetti bolognaise.

2007 Paul Conti Old Vine Grenache Shiraz $16

This is a powerful, full-flavoured red with dense concentrated dark berry characters, smooth texture and restrained oak and tannins. I'd like a bit more flesh but try with a robust, hearty, slow-cooked lamb shank dish.

2007 Peter Lehmann 'Seven Surveys' Shiraz Mourvedre Grenache $16.50

This has now been given the 'Seven Surveys' moniker and should be readily available on special. It's a very soft, easy-drinking red with ripe plummy fruit and plenty of tannins. I'd be thinking sirloin steak, onions, chips, and a side salad to keep the peace.

2006 Pikes 'Red Mullet' $14.95

This is not the new haircut that the Pikes' boys have taken a shine to; rather the third vintage of their unique red blend – of shiraz, mourvedre, tempranillo and grenache. It's uncomplicated, supple and easy to like, with dark berry flavours and restrained oak and tannins. A pretty good quaffer but I'd be drinking it with meat, not fish.

SHIRAZ CABERNET BLENDS

Shiraz cabernet blends are a unique Australian red wine style and include some of our great wines: Penfolds 'Bin 389', Yalumba 'Signature', Majella 'Mallaea', McWilliams '1877', Tapanappa 'Whalebone' and Wynns 'Johnsons Block'. All but four Penfolds Granges have included a small amount of cabernet to go with its shiraz – although it might be stretching the point to call it a shiraz cabernet blend.

This blend is considered unfashionable because it blends a grape from the French region of Bordeaux (cabernet) with one from the Rhône Valley (shiraz). The French can't blend these varieties legally in most parts of the country – although rumour suggests that it was common practice in Bordeaux in earlier times. Anyway, the blend works well in Australia, especially with quaffing wines such as those reviewed here.

Buying and Drinking Shiraz Cabernet Blends – A Tip

Drink now

From time to time we have found shiraz cabernets for less than $15 that deserved to be cellared. I suspect that this is becoming a thing of the past, and you'll need to pay more to find wines that are richer and more concentrated with firm finishes or substantial tannins. So I'm recommending that you drink the reds in this chapter as soon as it suits you. Of course, there are some wines here – the 2005 Bleasdale Shiraz Cabernet or the 2006 Elderton 'E' Shiraz Cabernet – that could be happily aged for anything from six months to two years. A short period in the coolest, darkest part of your house could well see you rewarded with wines that have been softened and are more ready to drink. If you haven't done this before, be sure to monitor any wines you put down by drinking one from time to time. But I'm not sure that I'd bother.

▬ BLOODY GOOD

2007 Banrock Station Shiraz Cabernet $9

The red winemakers from Constellation got this right. It's vibrant with ripe concentrated flavours, silky tongue-coating texture, and balance between its rich fruit, oak and tannins. Delicious.

2005 Bleasdale Shiraz Cabernet $14

The historic Langhorne Creek winery of the Potts family is making some terrific reds at a range of prices. This is jam-packed with rich, concentrated dark berry fruit flavours, has supple fleshy texture, and good length. It's drinking well now.

2006 Elderton 'E' Shiraz Cabernet $13.95

This is the style that made the Barossa famous, a robust red that is lush, fleshy and deeply concentrated, showing admirable balance between fruit, oak and tannins. Good, affordable drinking.

2006 Jacobs Creek Shiraz Cabernet $10.95

An excellent vintage of the cornerstone of the mighty Jacobs Creek range: ripe mulberry and blackcurrant flavours that are rich and concentrated, fleshy texture before a vibrant finish featuring supple, tight-knit tannins.

★ 2007 Queen Adelaide 'Regency Red' Shiraz Cabernet $8.95

THE QUAFF 2009 'Sausages and Chips'
BEST RED WINE UNDER $10 AWARD

This is remarkably good and a surprise packet. It's soft, round and fleshy with smooth texture and a pleasing juici-ness, ripe blackberry and dark plum flavours before a soft, gentle finish. Quaff on!

▶ GOOD

2007 De Bortoli 'Sacred Hill' Shiraz Cabernet $6.95

Another beauty from the team at De Bortoli under the 'Sacred Hill' label. This is nicely concentrated with lively dark berry fruit and restrained oak and tannins. It is smooth and easy to drink, with more flavour than most in the under-$10 market.

2006 Penfolds 'Koonunga Hill' Shiraz Cabernet $15.95

This is a well-made red from Penfolds that is soft, round and fleshy with deep blackcurrant and black plum flavours made approachable by its manageable tannins.

2006 Poet's Corner Shiraz Cabernet $9.95

This was originally a Mudgee brand that celebrated the area's local poet, Henry Lawson. He's probably spinning in his grave after the closure of the *Bulletin* so he won't be worrying about the change of focus with Poet's Corner. It's a hip brand that makes very good budget-priced wine – let's be happy with that. This has rich, briary dark berry and liquorice flavours, is supple and round in the mid-palate and has a pleasant finish. A good everyday drink at a fair price.

2006 Trentham Estate 'Murphy's Lore' Shiraz Cabernet $10

Currently the best wine from the Trentham entry-level range, this is super smooth, rich and concentrated with ripe mulberry, brambles and blackcurrant flavours before a gentle finish. Quaff on!

▶ PRETTY GOOD

2005 Deep Woods 'Ebony' Cabernet Shiraz $14.95

Deep Woods is a property from the northern areas of Margaret River near Yallingup being revitalised by Peter Fogarty, whose family owns Millbrook and Lake's Folly. This is supple, round and structured with some fleshiness, deep mulberry and other dark fruit flavours and restrained tannins.

2006 Dividing Range Shiraz Cabernet $10

This is one of the labels of the Victorian Alps winery and usually offers decent value. The wine is soft, round and fleshy with good concentration of redcurrant and blackberry flavours, if a tad firm to finish.

2006 Fool's Bay 'Beached' Shiraz Cabernet $14.95

This is from Hentley Farm in the Barossa and has rich, concentrated, ripe blackberry and dark plum flavours, fleshy almost syrupy texture, and a supple, balanced finish.

2006 Fox Creek 'Shadow's Run' Shiraz Cabernet $12

This has the generosity that you'd expect of a McLaren Vale red blend, some briary dark berry flavours, smooth though a bit syrupy, with plenty of oak and tannins yet still approachable.

2005 Jim Barry Shiraz Cabernet $14.95

A Clare quaffer that is soft, round, juicy and very easy drinking.

2005 Rouge Homme Shiraz Cabernet $16.95

Fruit for this label is being sourced from the Limestone Coast: it's soft, round and juicy – an easy-drinking style.

2006 Sandalford 'Element' Shiraz Cabernet $14

This is a Western Australian blend from one of the state's best wineries: ripe dark berry flavours, lively, juicy and pleasantly approachable.

OTHER RED BLENDS

There is an even greater diversity among the wines is this section than I usually find in my tastings for *Quaff*. Too many of the other red blends are bin ends – whatever is left over at the end of vintage. Not surprisingly, these are only occasionally successful. Fortunately, those reviewed below have been carefully blended to produce a style that the winemaker believes will appeal to consumers. Good examples of the latter are the 'Sero' red blends of De Bortoli Chief Winemaker, Steve Webber, whose experimentation continues to provide some of the most exciting wines on the market. Some winemakers have succeeded in finding a style that suits their region and are consistently producing excellent quaffing wines – albeit with unusual blends.

The best of the other red blends tend to have deep dark berry flavours, smooth texture and soft, fine, ripe, restrained tannins, and show balance between their fruit and the oak treatment they receive. Obviously, the key to this is the amount and quality of oak used in their production. As a general rule with these wines, when the oak is held back, the fruit shines.

Consumers seem to prefer straight varietals (especially shiraz and merlot) and these are currently easier to sell than blends. A look at the wine recommended following suggests that because red blends are unfashionable, they can be bargains.

The reliables –
consistent-quality wines, year in, year out

Peter Lehmann 'Clancy's' has been in all but one edition of *Quaff* and
is the only wine featured in this section with such an extensive record
for consistency.

> ## Buying and Drinking Other Red Blends –
> ## Some Tips
>
> ### Labelling blends
> By Australian law, wine may be labelled a straight varietal if it
> contains 85% or more of that grape variety. If a blend has more
> than 15% of another variety (or varieties), it (or they) must be
> named. For example, a wine that is 60% cabernet sauvignon,
> 30% merlot and 10% petit verdot may be labelled cabernet
> merlot – or cabernet merlot petit verdot.
>
> The order in which the grape varieties appear on a label indi-
> cates which variety makes the largest contribution to the
> blend. So a shiraz merlot cabernet will be mostly shiraz, with
> the smallest part of the blend being cabernet.
>
> ### Drink now
> These are reds made for early consumption. You'll notice that
> most of those reviewed are from the 2006 and 2007 vintages.
> They'll still be drinking well in a year or two but won't be
> improved by cellaring. Many have a slight tannic grip on the
> finish. Consume these with a slow-cooked lamb roast, a hearty
> beef casserole or some spicy sausages and they'll slip down
> with the greatest of ease.

◣ BLOODY GOOD

2006 De Bortoli 'Sero' Merlot Sangiovese $14.20

This is an intriguing red that has dense, concentrated dark berry characters with some savoury notes, almost velvety texture, layers of flavour, a juicy succulence before you get hit by a substantial tannin whack. It's balanced and needs a rustic Italian dish like osso buco to put things in perspective.

2005 Shenton Ridge Classic Red $7.50

I wrote in my weekly *STM* column, 'I've learnt to expect the unexpected in Margaret River, so I shouldn't have been surprised.' Up pops this little number from a producer whom I didn't know. From a vineyard in the northern reaches of the region, in the old potato-growing area of Jindong – it is flat, fertile, has plentiful irrigation and makes very good quaffing red of decent quality. I wrote my tasting notes, found out the identity of the wine and its price. Unbelievable. Anyway, this is soft, round and smooth with blackcurrant and redcurrant flavours, power, and some elegance before a fresh, clean, gentle finish. Great drinking. Quaff on!

2006 Thorn Clarke 'Sandpiper' The Blend $15

This is an unlikely blend of shiraz, petit verdot and caber-net from the Barossa. It works well, producing a densely concentrated red with redcurrant and black plum flavours, smooth texture and a fresh, clean, balanced finish. Uncomplicated but flavoursome.

2006 Zonte's Footstep Cabernet Malbec $15

This Langhorne Creek producer has been having a pretty tough time with the drought and the poor flow of the Murray decimating its water supply. Here's another of the terrific reds that they deliver with pleasing regularity. It has ripe, sweet fruit (blackberries, mulberries), silky smooth texture and complementary, fine-knit tannins.

➤ GOOD

2006 Nepenthe 'Tryst' Cabernet Tempranillo Zinfandel $16.95

This Adelaide Hills winery is now part of the McGuigan Simeon group and is pumping out more wine than before. What I've seen has been decent quaffing wine – readily discounted – so I've no complaints. This is a crazy blend but Nepenthe does a madly attractive wild berry zin and this does work. It's soft and round with ripe, sweet fruit – redcurrants and blackberries – and smooth texture before smooth yet balanced tannins.

2005 Peter Lehmann 'Clancy's' Shiraz Cabernet Merlot $15

This is just the style my wife, Elaine, loves: it's robust, oaky, bold and full-flavoured. There are heaps of dense, concentrated red berry fruits, good texture and moderate tannins. It's approachable now, thought I'd be looking for something that was also pretty robust: a slow-cooked oxtail stew or lamb shanks. (No need to worry, I'm allowed my fair share of the reds at the evening meal.)

➤ PRETTY GOOD

2007 Jacobs Creek 'Three Vines' Shiraz Cabernet Tempranillo $15

This is good current drinking: sweet, ripe briary flavours and smooth texture. A good spaghetti and meatballs dish with a tomato-based sauce would soften the finish nicely.

2006 Peel Estate Premium Red $14.95

Will Nairn's Peel is a favourite winery less than an hour's drive from Perth, always with a warm welcome. This is a blend of shiraz, merlot, cabernet franc, cabernet sauvignon and touriga – as I said, a bin-end blend. It's drinking well – bright, lively redcurrant and red cherry flavours with a gentle tannin whack.

2004 Scarpantoni 'School Block' Shiraz Cabernet Merlot $14.95

> This will divide opinion. Some will love the voluminous coconutty oak which dominates the wine while others will look for more restraint. Make your choice.

2007 Wolf Blass 'Eaglehawk' Shiraz Merlot Cabernet $9.95

> A pleasant light- to medium-bodied red that shows ripe, sweet fruit, is smooth and juicy with some grip to finish.

Sunstone Luscious Fruity Red $9.95

> This is a non-vintage sweet red from the Riverina and McWilliams: it's ripe, grapey and very fruity (my notes said exuberantly so). While it's a bit sweet for me, it's clean and fresh and plenty will love it.

The honey wind blows

Sweet wines under $15

SWEET WINES UNDER $15

There are three sections to this short chapter: 'sweet wines' – the fresher, lighter styles made from late-harvest aromatic grapes, such as muscat, verdelho, riesling and chenin; 'sweet reds' (which has become 'sweet red'); and 'very sweet wines' – the lush dessert wines (or stickies), which are made from much riper, more sugary, shrivelled grapes. Usually, stickies are made from semillon or riesling although the hybrid grape taminga makes the occasional noteworthy sticky. Generally, the grapes for these have been infected with 'noble rot' (*Botrytis cinerea*) – and I'm suggesting in the title of this chapter that it can happen as a result of a 'honey wind blowing'. The noble rot speeds up the shrivelling and concentrates the grape sugars. This has the effect of significantly sweetening and concentrating the wines and contributes a rich apricot and marmalade flavour to them. Botrytis wines are expensive to produce, which is why so few are featured here: the best are wonderful bargains. There are a couple of Australia's best stickies, too, reviewed in the Great-Value Wines over $15 chapter (see page 200).

The reliables –
consistent-quality wines, year in, year out

Once again, Brown Brothers has shown itself to be the most consistent producer of Australian sweet wines under $15. Its classic sweetie, Brown Brothers Lexia (originally Spatlese Lexia), has appeared in each edition of *Quaff*, while the Orange Muscat & Flora and the sweet red, Dolcetto Syrah, are represented here again. The latter continues the improvement it showed last year. The Brown Brothers Moscato (reviewed in the chapter on sweet sparkling wines on page 41) has made all but one edition of *Quaff* and was our first Wine of the Year. The first vintage of the sweet sparkling 'Zibibbo' was last year's *Quaff* Sparkling Wine of the Year but the current vintage, although pretty good, is less convincing.

Buying and Drinking Sweet Wines – Some Tips

Drink young
Fruitiness and sweetness go hand in hand and so the best time to drink these sweet wines is while they are young, vibrant and fruity – at the stage when their primary flavours are at their peak. Drink slightly chilled and enjoy.

Matching sweet wines with food
How do you decide what dessert you will serve with these sweet wines? It depends entirely on how light or heavy the wine is. The simple rule is that the lighter and less sweet the wine is, the lighter and less sweet the dessert should be. Conversely, the heavier and sweeter the wine, the sweeter the dessert should be.

So with the sweet wines, try fruit salad, pavlova or fruit-based soufflés, and with the very sweet wines, heavier desserts such as crème brûlée, bread and butter pudding or sticky date pudding.

All you need is a half bottle
One of the ways in which you can tell the difference between sweet and very sweet wine is that the latter is invariably sold in half bottles. On most occasions, a half bottle of dessert wine will be enough for a dinner party. It is sweeter and richer than a full bottle of table wine or even sweet wine. And at the time of the meal when we serve stickies, our appetites are beginning to flag.

Sweet Wines

 **BLOODY GOOD**

2007 Brown Brothers Lexia $12.90
This is one of the reliables (called Spatlese Lexia in 2006) as it has been omnipresent in *Quaff*. There are the distinctive grapey aromatics that you expect with lexia, but in 2007 it's quite dramatic. The flavours are full-on and sweet while the texture is soft and silky before it finishes clean, crisp and fresh.

2008 Brown Brothers Orange Muscat & Flora $14
This is an excellent vintage for this old favourite: delightfully fragrant fresh flowers, attractive sweet apricot and lime flavours, light to medium body, and soft cleansing acidity.

 **PRETTY GOOD**

McWilliams 'Inheritance' Fruitwood $6.95
While it's too sweet for me, there are pleasant grapey aromas, a smooth texture and a clean fresh finish.

2007 Trentham Estate 'Murphy's Lore' Spatlese Lexia $10
Light-bodied, sweet with attractive grapey flavours. For those with a sweet tooth.

Sweet Red

➤ BLOODY GOOD

2008 Brown Brothers Dolcetto Syrah $15.40

This massive seller from Brown Brothers appears to be getting better every year. In the past, I've loved its aromatics but found it too sweet and cloying. No such problem with the last two vintages at least. There's those sweet wild berries, mulberries, brambles, lavish sweetness in the mid-palate and clean crisp cleansing finish. A crowd pleaser – but I can see why.

Very Sweet Wines

▄► BLOODY GOOD

2006 De Bortoli 'Deen Vat 5' Botrytis Semillon $12.95 (375 ml)

There's little difference quality-wise between the 2005 and 2006 vintages of this terrific, amazing-value-for-money botrytis semillon. It is lighter of body than the Noble One and less densely packed with fruit flavour. I don't find that a problem. I loved the Vat 5's finesse and lightness of touch, especially when it's accompanied by intense honey, apricot and lemon curd characters, excellent balance and clean, crisp finish.

2006 Vintage Cellars Botrytis Semillon $9.95 (375 ml)

This own-label sticky from Vintage Cellars is up a quality notch on the previous vintage. It is soft, round and fine, has intense apricot and peach flavour, lush creamy texture and some fresh limey, lemony acidity to cleanse the palate. Delicious and great value. Exclusive to Vintage Cellars.

▄► GOOD

2003 Trentham Estate Noble Taminga $12.50 (375 ml)

Written up in last year's *Quaff*, still available and still drinking well. Following in the footsteps of the awesomely good 2002 means that we can expect this sticky to age beautifully also. Certainly it's in great shape for a five-year-old sweetie from the Murray–Darling. There's heaps of lush, sweet honey, apricot, grapefruit and marmalade characters, as well as good depth of flavour before a finish that is very sweet but not cloying.

The unfashionably great

Aussie fortifieds under $15

AUSSIE FORTIFIEDS UNDER $15

While it's clear that the world of Australian fortified wines under $15 is not littered with bargains, as it once was, there are still plenty of quality wines at bedrock prices in this chapter. The best of them are world class – you won't find better fortifieds anywhere at comparable prices. However, there is less than optimum consistency among our fortifieds and, frankly, plenty of wines are to be avoided. The slow-down in sales means that some stocks are not kept as fresh as they would be in an ideal world. No such problems with those rated in this chapter.

The disappointing news is that production of fortifieds continues to decline – down to 8.0 million litres, 37% lower than 2005/2006. Sales have fallen too, from 18.5 million litres in 2006 to 17.4 million litres in 2007, a drop of 6%. Fortifieds now represent only 3.6% of domestic sales.

THE QUAFF 2009 'Any Port In a Storm'
FORTIFIED WINE OF THE YEAR AWARD

On the shortlist for this award are:
De Bortoli 'Show' Liqueur Muscat
Penfolds 'Club Reserve' Aged Tawny
Taminick Cellars Liqueur Muscat
The six-times champ, Penfolds 'Club Reserve' Aged Tawny, is still a remarkable quaffing wine and a brilliant drink. I can't believe that it's not more popular than it is. The muscat class is very strong: Taminick has been making more effort with marketing and is now getting its bargain-priced wines out and about. I love the different flavour profile of this liqueur muscat: it's unforgettable. Yet, I've decided to give the *Quaff 2009* 'Any Port in a Storm' Fortified Wine of the Year to the **De Bortoli 'Show' Liqueur Muscat**, for its pure varietal character, opulence, incredible lush texture and impeccable balance.

The reliables –
consistent-quality wines, year in, year out

The only two fortified wines to have appeared in every edition of *Quaff* are the two Penfolds gems: the 'Club' Tawny and the 'Club Reserve' Aged Tawny. Between them – and under slightly different names (Penfolds 'Club' Port and Penfolds 'Reserve' Bin 421) – they have won most of our fortified awards. The 'Club Reserve' Aged Tawny has never been rated below 'Bloody Good', an outstanding achievement. The big improver in this section in the last couple of years has been Angoves; the turnaround we noted last year has continued, especially with the 'Bookmark' range.

Buying and Drinking Fortified Wines – Some Tips

Unfashionable, therefore cheap

Tougher drink-driving laws and great consciousness of drinking in moderation are partly responsible for fortified wines becoming unfashionable. This has meant that many of the wines in this chapter are available at bargain-basement prices. It has also meant that some wine lovers are paying more for fortifieds but drinking less of them.

Plan your dinner party to include fortifieds

One of the reasons for fortifieds losing their appeal is that appetites often wane before we reach the stage of the meal where they come into their own. Plan to drink a freshly opened, slightly chilled dry sherry as an aperitif – with either freshly shucked oysters or lightly grilled prawns. For dessert, serve an opulent muscat with a paneforte-style cake (such as New Norcia Nut Cake) or a flourless chocolate cake with an intense tawny and a short black.

Port

BLOODY GOOD

Penfolds 'Club Reserve' Aged Tawny $14.95

It's the same old story. There were three of us around the tasting bench: the scores uniformly high for this wine, and almost as high for the next. I wonder idly what the wine is – you tend not to guess when you're tasting blind. I don't have a clue but this is good. When all is revealed, there's no surprise. So when I say, 'Remarkably consistent and still superb after all these years,' you had better believe it. I wondered about the depth of the Penfolds 'Club Reserve' in *Quaff 2008*. No such reservations in 2009. It is soft, round and easy drinking, rich, concentrated toffee, treacle, caramel and honey flavours that are wonderfully sweet, all impeccably balanced by fine spirit before a long, gentle finish. This seamless fortified is a stunning wine for the price.

Penfolds 'Club' Tawny $11.95

This is much better than last year's 'Club' Tawny, having rich treacle and honey flavours, silky smooth texture and a balanced, fine finish that is soft and delicate. Back to form.

GOOD

Bleasdale 'Wise One' Port $16

This Langhorne Creek winery has a long history of producing classy fortifieds and so it's no surprise to see its budget-priced tawny looking good. There are malty toffee, treacle and honey flavours that are rich and intense – plenty of power, just a tad short to finish. Delicious anyway.

Grant Burge Aged Tawny $16.30

> There were some complex rancio characters on the nose that meant the wine was better after a vigorous swirl and even better on the palate than the nose. There are earthy, mushroomy, toffee characters before a long, dry finish.

McWilliams Hanwood 'Classic' Tawny $11.95

> This is bigger, deeper, richer than last year, sweet and concentrated with toffee, treacle flavours and a gentle, soft finish.

Sherry

▶ BLOODY GOOD

Angoves 'Bookmark' Dry Sherry $5.95

> This is one of the remarkable bargains in *Quaff*, even though its price has shot up an unbelievable 20% (by a dollar). Not only is it impossibly cheap but it's a decent sherry. There are some salty, nutty, rancio characters on the nose while the wine is very fine and intense with a dry finish that lingers.

McWilliams 'Hanwood' Amontillado Sherry $10.95

> Amontillado is a style of sherry that begins as a fino, has lost the influence of the flor yeast and become richer, deeper and darker than the fino. This is fragrant, soft, round and plump with a hint of toffee and dried fruits before a gentle, dry finish.

▶ GOOD

Angoves 'Bookmark' Cream Sherry $5.95

> There's some toffee, lime juice, cooked orange peel and honey filling out the sweet mid-palate before a clean, soft finish.

Angoves 'Bookmark' Medium Sherry $5.95

> This is gently sweet, supple, round and plump, with fine, gentle spirit before a pleasant, soft finish.

McWilliams Medium Dry Sherry $6.95

> No question that this is easy to like: sweet butterscotch, toffee and treacle flavours and a sweetish finish.

▶ PRETTY GOOD

McWilliams Cream Sherry $6.95

> It's very sweet and syrupy with sweet, lush, grapey flavours. Pour on top of the ice-cream.

Muscat and Tokay

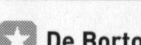 **BLOODY GOOD**

⭐ De Bortoli 'Show' Liqueur Muscat $14.95
THE QUAFF 2009 'Any Port In a Storm'
FORTIFIED WINE OF THE YEAR AWARD

I said last year, 'This is stunningly good: a Riverina fortified that at this price point matches it with the best of Rutherglen,' and I'll stick with that view having seen the current wine. It's powerful, rich and concentrated, with raisiny, treacle, molasses and liquorice flavours, lush texture and a neatly balanced finish that lingers. Unbelievable value.

Morris 'Black Label' Liqueur Muscat $11.95

This is the third year in a row that I've said, 'You won't find a better Rutherglen muscat for less than $15,' and this year I added, 'Gosh, it's good.' David Morris continues to craft substantial volumes of this beguiling fortified. There's a finesse about this muscat: deep gentle raisin, toffee, molasses flavours, satiny smooth and lush texture, a lingering aftertaste. A classy winter warmer that is almost as good as an electric blanket.

Taminick Cellars Liqueur Muscat $14

Wow! The unassuming Taminick Cellars at Glenrowan has produced a stunning muscat. What makes this different is its amazing floral fragrance, its touch of dried herbs, wild honey, thyme: there's a seductive edge to the velvety smooth, lush, butterscotch and toffee flavours. It's beautifully fresh and seamless. Quaff on!

PS

Angoves 'Bookmark' Marsala $5.95

This is the second year in a row that I've been so impressed with this fortified. There's pure vanilla essence leaping out of the glass and then those seductive caramel and dark butterscotch flavours, and lush texture before an attractive refreshing finish that is long and sweet. It is very sweet, yet balanced, and I suspect dangerously easy to drink.

Maxwell Liqueur Mead $19

This remains the pick of Maxwell's three meads: I like its softness, silky viscous texture, honey, nutmeg and clove flavours and clean finish in which the fruit and spirit are balanced.

Maxwell Spiced Mead $12

I visited Maxwell for the first time this year and Mark Maxwell explained that the Spiced Mead was supposed to be warmed, like mulled wine. Ah, now I get it! And winter evenings may never be the same.

Stones Green Ginger Wine $8.95

With the Stones entry, I usually say, 'Some things never change.' Certainly the wine is the same as ever with its lively ginger-beer aromas, softness, sweetness and ability to avoid being cloying. But what is different this year is that my wife grabbed the bottle and said, 'This is just what I need for my cold.' I noticed the level dropping quickly over the next week. 'It's very therapeutic,' explained Elaine.

The foreign legion

Imported wines under $20

IMPORTED WINES
UNDER $20

More so than ever before Vintage Cellars has dominated the budget-priced imported wine scene, as it brings increasing numbers of everyday wines into the country. Restaurants have more imported wines available than before, although at higher price points. South American wine is better represented than before. New Zealand continues to be well represented in this chapter, for although most Kiwi wines tend to be priced above $20 a bottle, the large companies do have some excellent quaffing wines.

The strength of this chapter can be seen in the substantial number of 'Bloody Goods' and the scarcity of 'Pretty Goods' in the rating of these wines. There's something here for everybody – and a few screaming bargains to be had for canny lovers or followers of *Quaff*.

Previously, I've justified the $20 price point for this chapter by explaining that there is a great deal available between $15 and $20 from overseas wineries and only a limited amount under $15, so the $20 price point works better for these wines. This still holds, except for some bargain-basement-priced wines from the large chains.

For contact details of each importer, refer to the section 'Finding the Wines' on page 209.

THE QUAFF 2009 'A Foreign Affair'
EXOTIC WHITE WINE OF THE YEAR

On the shortlist for this award are:

Ombra Prosecco
2007 Corte Giara Pinot Grigio delle Venezie
2007 Bodega Norton Torrontes

Here we have two wines from the north-east of Italy: the Ombra Prosecco, a well-priced dry sparkling in a style that is seen too rarely in Australia, and the Corte Giara Pinot Grigio, a good example of a style of white wine that is proving popular in this country. The Argentinian torrontes is something completely different, although the style will appear familiar to those who find gewurztraminer and muscat of Alexandria fascinating. There's a wonderful aromaticity there. In a tight contest, I'll give the nod to the **2007 Corte Giara Pinot Grigio delle Venezie**. Try it as a contrast with some of the Aussie pinot gris and pinot grigios that are available in abundance.

THE QUAFF 2009 'Another Foreign Affair'
EXOTIC RED WINE OF THE YEAR

On the shortlist for this award are:

2006 Aradon Rioja
2005 Casa Santos 'Quinta das Setencostas'
2006 Altos Las Hormigas 'Colonia Las Liebres' Bonarda

This pits two wines from the Iberian Peninsula against the Spanish-speaking Argentinians. The Rioja is a fabulous modern style of tempranillo from a famous region, while the wildly popular Portuguese red is a good example of why there's been such a revival of red table wines in that country. The Argentinian red shows how well the Piedmontese variety bonarda has settled into its new environment. These are all well-priced quaffers that will help extend our love affair with wine by showing that there is plenty that is new and exciting in the world of wine. In a tight contest, I'll go for the **2006 Aradon Rioja** because of its succulence and approachability: it's just so easy to like.

The reliables –
consistent-quality wines, year in, year out

Of the Reliables which have featured in earlier editions of *Quaff*, only Montana from New Zealand is present this year (Stoneleigh's Pinot Gris has crept up in price, and is now in the Great-Value Wines Over $15 chapter). The Geisen Sauvignon Blanc and the Concha Y Toro 'Casillero del Diablo', Arrogant Frog and Portone labels may well be heading for Reliable status.

Buying and Drinking Imported Wines – Some Tips

Expanding horizons

There can't be many readers of this book who don't regularly eat in restaurants or cafes that feature a range of different cuisines – Italian, Greek, French, Chinese, Thai, Vietnamese ... And I'll bet that the majority of us cook dishes from lots of different countries. We all love something different, a new taste experience, something to tantalise. Trying imported wines is a bit like that, broadening one's horizons, learning a bit more about the infinite possibilities that wine offers. One of the things that I love when I'm overseas is trying the local wines. Being able to enjoy them when I'm back in Australia helps rekindle those memories – as well as providing an opportunity for me to try something different.

Wine without food – not in Europe

Most of the wines from countries such as France, Italy, Spain, Portugal and Greece are just made to go with food. In these places, grapes have been grown for hundreds of years and a local cuisine has grown up alongside the region's wines. They can sometimes look pretty ordinary when tasted by them-selves, but are transformed with food. You might also like to try appropriate food and wine from the same country: an albarino from Galacia with a seafood paella; a French Provençale stew with a hearty red from the Minervois; a bone-dry rosé from the Côtes du Rhône with a salmon fillet; your perfect spaghetti bolognaise with a rustic nero d'avola.

Imported Sparkling

━━ **BLOODY GOOD**

Henkell Trocken $17.95

I can't remember this dry bubbly from Germany's Rhine Valley tasting as delicious as this: it's fresh, clean and lively with yeasty, biscuity characters, soft, creamy texture and a gentle, fine finish. Imported by McWilliams.

Ombra Prosecco $15.95

I'd say the best marketing I've ever seen was that done in Italy for the fizzy, dry, semi-sparkling wine made in the Veneto of the indigenous variety, prosecco. It seemed that every restaurant I went into north of Rome, the first thing that happened is that I was greeted with a glass containing a mouthful of prosecco. I became very used to this delicious aperitif. Vallis Mareni makes a pleasant prosecco under the Ombra label: it's light, fine and intense with some yeasty, bready, lemony flavours and a crisp, dry finish. Exclusive to Vintage Cellars.

NV Segura Viudas Aria Brut Nature $16.95

A delightfully different sparkling wine – a cava from Spain's Penedes (near Barcelona), made from three local varieties (macabeo, xarel-lo, parellada): very soft and creamy, delicate, pure and fine with a crisp, dry finish that satisfies. Imported by Bacardi Lion.

NV Segura Viudas Semiseco $13.95

This semiseco ('semi-dry' – meaning sweet) bubbly is quite delicious: fragrant, fine and intensely fruity with sweet rose-petal and grapey flavours before a fresh, clean finish. Carefully balanced. Imported by Bacardi Lion.

Imported Whites

■► BLOODY GOOD

2007 Bodega Norton Torrontes $9.95

This privately owned winery in Mendoza was established by an Englishman in 1895 (which is why you can pronounce its name) and is now owned by an Austrian. Torrontes is the name given to three different white grape varieties found in Argentina and linked to muscat. That's what this delightfully aromatic white reminds me most of. It's morning-dew fresh, riotously floral, with rose-petal and muscaty grape flavours, sensuously viscous, finishing clean and fresh. Brilliant. Exclusive to Vintage Cellars.

2006 Burgans Albarino $16.95

This is a very good example of albarino, a brilliant Spanish varietal that has a deserved cult following in Europe and is usually much more expensive than this. The Burgans label is produced by Bodegas Martin Codax, a cooperative of grapegrowers in Rias Baixas (far north-west Spain) that is Spain's largest producer of albarino, and is sealed under screwcap (yeah!). There are some freshly cut mountain flowers, honey and melon aromas, while the palate is fresh, clean and minerally with some chalky, slatey flavours that linger. Exclusive to Vintage Cellars.

2007 Casa Silva 'Reserva' Sauvignon Blanc $18.80

From a long-established family winery based in Chile's Colchagua Valley, this is very dry and textural, not at all fruity, more minerally and savoury and with fine, gentle acidity. Different and worth trying. Imported by Grape Expectations.

⭐ **2007 Corte Giara Pinot Grigio delle Venezie** $17.95

THE QUAFF 2009 'A Foreign Affair'
EXOTIC WHITE WINE OF THE YEAR

The Allegrini family's Corte Giara sources the grapes for this from the Veneto in north-eastern Italy, from the hills facing picturesque Lake Garda. This is a leap up in quality from the previous vintage: bright and fresh with intense savoury characters, good viscosity and a crisp dry finish. Classic pinot grigio. Imported by Negociants.

2007 Giesen Sauvignon Blanc $19.50

There's a reason that this is one of the best-selling of the Marlborough sauvignons: it's a great example of the style and has excellent fruit definition. Crammed with ripe, intense gooseberry and lychee flavours and finishing with a burst of tingling passionfruit. Nicely clean cut and refreshing. Imported by Negociants.

2007 Kono Sauvignon Blanc $11.95

Kono is the first Maori family brand selling to the retail trade. The Konos are based in Nelson and also market seafood, fruit and honey. This Marlborough sauvignon is sourced from their vineyards in the Awatere, Waihopai and Wairau Valleys. There's plenty of persistent gooseberry and lychee flavours, good weight and a tight, fine structure that enables the wine to linger on the palate. Imported by Dan Murphy's.

2007 Montana Sauvignon Blanc $19.50

While Montana makes buckets of this Marlborough sauvignon – 700,000 cases on the way to 900,000 – its technical skill, rigour, attention to detail and careful sourcing of fruit enables it to produce a quality wine at a decent price. This has some minerally characters on the nose and a passionfruit lift in the mid-palate, accompanied by heaps of intense tropical flavours before a gentle crisp finish. Imported by Pernod Ricard.

Oisly & Thesee 'Les Nuages' Loire Sauvignon Blanc $11.95

This is a regional sauvignon from the Oisly et Thesee co-operative based in Touraine in the Loire. It's such a different style from Australian and New Zealand sauvignon blanc and so well worth trying. It's delicately fragrant, plump and delicious, and quite textural before tight crisp acidity cleanses the palate. Exclusive to Vintage Cellars.

2006 Portone Soave $7.95

Soaves are refreshing, unoaked whites from the Veneto in north-eastern Italy, made from the garganega grape with a little trebbiano. This is a merchant's label from a large co-operative that is surprising me by looking better with age. Tasted in July, it was still fresh and clean with some fresh talc and anise aromas, chalky, savoury characters and lively minerality to finish. A great place to start an exploration of classic Italian whites. Exclusive to Vintage Cellars.

Imported Rosés

📌 **PRETTY GOOD**

2007 Arrogant Frog Ribet Pink $9.95

Sourced from the Languedoc-Roussillon in the South of France by a marketing savvy, Arrogant Frog. Made (by a humble winemaker!) from syrah, this is soft, round and supple with ripe, sweet strawberry flavours that linger. Exclusive to Vintage Cellars.

Imported Reds

BLOODY GOOD

2006 Altos Las Hormigas 'Colonia Las Liebres' Bonarda $14

Although bonarda was originally from Piedmont in northern Italy, it appears to have taken on a new lease of life in Argentina. This wine is sourced from the Mendoza Valley and is a terrific quaffer: ripe, plummy and vibrant with deep blackcurrant flavours and firm yet balanced tannins to finish. Imported by Grape Expectations.

2007 Altos Las Hormigas Malbec $17

Here is an impressive, well-priced red from the Mendoza region of Argentina: attractive blueberry flavours, silky smooth texture, very fine structure, delightfully approachable. Imported by Grape Expectations.

2006 Aradon Rioja $9.95

THE QUAFF 2009 'Another Foreign Affair'
EXOTIC RED WINE OF THE YEAR

This is a brilliantly priced, modern rioja: redcurrant and blackberry flavours that are sweet and ripe, silky smooth texture, and restrained, beautifully balanced tannins. Exclusive to Vintage Cellars.

2005 Casa Santos 'Quinta das Setencostas' $14.95

Sometimes a wine lover needs to know everything important about a wine. This is from a family winery in Alenquer (just north of Lisbon) and is a single-estate red blend of the indigenous Portuguese varieties periquita, camarate, tinta miuda and (as the Vintage Cellars lads say, 'the instantly recognisable') preto-martinho. On other occasions, you only need to know that it has been a runaway success for Vintage Cellars – and no wonder. It's a power-packed, densely flavoured red that has fabulous concentration, smooth, almost velvety texture, and balanced, fine-knit tannins. Needs a substantial dish: say grilled sirloin with a robust red-wine sauce. Bottled under screw-cap. Exclusive to Vintage Cellars.

2006 Dashwood Pinot Noir $19.95

Dashwood is the second label of Marlborough's Vavasour, which is based south of Blenheim in the cool Awatere Valley. This pinot has fresh, clean and juicy concentrated redcurrant flavours, good depth and power and a gently firm finish. Exclusive to Vintage Cellars.

2005 O Fournier 'Urban Uco' Malbec $17.00

O Fournier is based in Argentina's Mendoza and is making some smart wines. This is pleasantly fragrant, has ripe plummy, blackberry flavours with some extraction and just enough grip to remind you this is red wine. Imported by Grape Expectations.

 **GOOD**

2005 Bodega Norton Reserva Malbec $11.95

There's plenty of rich, concentrated, dark berry flavours in this Argentinian malbec. It's quite grippy to finish but still approachable. Exclusive to Vintage Cellars.

2006 Concha Y Toro 'Casillero del Diablo' Cabernet Sauvignon $13.95

From South America's largest wine producer – in the Central Valley of Chile – a decent follow-up to the 2005 cabernet: this is soft and round with deep, rich, concentrated dark berry flavours, a pleasing mouthfeel, before a finish that features substantial, balanced tannins. Exclusive to Vintage Cellars.

2007 Cono Sur Pinot Noir $9.95

The pun is so awful that I'm not sure I can ever forgive them. The large-scale winery is based at Chimbarongo in Chile's Colchagua Valley and, judging by the pictures on the website, it's very much state of the art. Still, it's a decent pinot – especially at the price. There's a delightful softness, some varietal character – strawberry and dark cherry flavours, smooth texture – and a pleasant mouthfeel before a gentle finish. Exclusive to Vintage Cellars.

2005 M Chapoutier 'La Ciboise' Coteaux de Tricastin $16.95

Chapoutier is one of the great family names of the Rhône. This is from a small appellation between the southern and northern Rhône, Côteaux de Tricastin, and is a fruit-driven style made primarily from grenache. It has earthy, gravelly, dark berry and blackcurrant flavours, very dry and savoury, with its finish dominated by powerful tannins. It needs a substantial beef stew, such as boeuf en daube, to look at its best. Imported by Fine Wine Wholesalers.

2007 Obikwa Shiraz $9.95

This South African red is a surprise packet and the pick of the wines under this label for me. It's from the country's second-largest wine producer, Distell. The label has been a huge hit for Coles, with a bottle sold in some Liquorland store every five seconds (what those guys can do with statistics!). Anyway, Australia is Obikwa's largest export market. This is fragrant, has rich, concentrated, deep dark berry flavours, silky smooth texture and a clean, fresh, balanced finish. Exclusive to Coles, Liquorland, Vintage Cellars.

◗ PRETTY GOOD

2006 Concha Y Toro 'Casillero del Diablo' Carmenère $13.95

Sourced from Chile's Rapel Valley and fleshed out by some cabernet (10%) and syrah (5%), here is a juicy, fruity, blackberry pastille-flavoured red of medium body that finishes quite firm and tannic. Exclusive to Vintage Cellars.

2007 Concha Y Toro 'Casillero del Diablo' Malbec $13.95

This is a powerful, robust Chilean red that is rich and concentrated with dark berry flavours and substantial tannins to finish. Exclusive to Vintage Cellars.

Lash out

Great-value wines over $15

GREAT-VALUE WINES OVER $15

Most people most of the time, either through necessity or choice, don't want to spend more than $15 on a bottle of wine. And that is clearly the focus of this book. However, there will be times when you can't resist the temptation to spend a bit more – it may be something you do for dinner on weekends or for special occasions, or you might share more expensive bottles with wine-loving friends to expand your knowledge of wines.

So this section of the book contains reviews of more than 100 wines that have a recommended retail price above the $15 limit. You'll find some of these on special below $15. Those that are more expensive will still represent very good value for money. In many cases, I saw them as part of the *Quaff* tastings – and found subsequently that they had a recommended retail price about $15. However, there are many outstanding bargains that I saw as part of my normal work as a wine writer – for *STM* (the *Sunday Times Magazine*) in Perth, *Gourmet Traveller Wine*, the *Qantas Magazine* and *Money Magazine*. I also conduct regular new-release tastings: when I'm home I taste 30 wines a night on Mondays, Tuesdays and Fridays.

As always with *Quaff*, I am recommending the crème de la crème, the wines that stood out – firstly for reasons of quality, and only secondly because they represent good value.

Buying Wines over $15 – Some Tips

On special

With changes on the Australian retail scene, especially connected with the expansion of Coles and Woolworths (under all their different shop fronts), nothing stays the same. Discounting and special deals are very much part of daily life. Keep an eye on newspaper advertising to see if any of the wines recommended here are available as specials. You may well find that some of the wines I believe are good value for $18–$20 are available on special under $15, and some that we recommended at $22–$25 are on sale for less than $20. There are no rules, especially with loss leaders. Most liquor stores have 20% (or more) sales on a couple of occasions during the year. Get to know when these are held.

Adopt a wine merchant

There are significant advantages in establishing a relationship with a wine merchant, especially a local one, and channelling all or most of your wine purchases through them. They'll certainly keep you informed of any special deals (whether on price or the availability of rare or difficult-to-get wines). If there are bargains, you'll hear about them first. If those bargains are in short supply, you can expect to be looked after. Another advantage is that the wine merchant will get to know your tastes and that will help them in recommending wines to you. Cultivate the friendship. Once you have found them, never let them go.

Sparkling Wines over $15

2007 Annie's Lane Moscato $19.95

This is very good indeed. There's a pink – even bronze – tinge. This light fizzy drop is delicately fruity, brightly fresh and pristine with restrained sweetness and zesty acidity.

Bay of Fires 'Tigress' Pinot Noir Chardonnay $22

Another superb bubbly from the Constellation group and Tasmania: it's delicate, very fine, has lightly yeasty flavours, creamy texture and a zippy, dry finish that lingers. Classy and well priced.

White Wines over $15

2007 Amberley Semillon Sauvignon Blanc $21.50

Another part of the Constellation empire is benefiting from improvements following the takeover. This is deliciously different from most Margaret River semillon sauvignon blancs, having pronounced green bean and snow pea flavours, and it is tight, lean and tangy with a dry, zesty finish.

2008 Cape Mentelle Sauvignon Blanc Semillon $27.95

This and the Grosset SBS are among the most expensive examples of the style in the country. What are they doing in a book that is concerned first and foremost with value for money? The reality is that they are a stunning example of the blend, they're scene-setters and, while not cheap, represent good value. Try them if you spot them served by the glass in a restaurant and you'll see what I mean. The Cape Mentelle is wonderfully youthful and fresh, has vibrant zesty flavours, plump juiciness, grassy, tropical flavours, and a long tangy finish that lingers.

2007 Celestial Bay Chardonnay $19.95

This is a new Margaret River property with a large Wilyabrup vineyard. While it is likely to make better cabernet than chardonnay in the long run, it is currently offering a decent Margaret River chardonnay at a very attractive price. The 2007 is soft, round and fleshy with ripe peachy melony flavours of good concentration and a lively, powerful finish.

2007 Cockfighters Ghost Semillon $18.50

There's renewed effort in the Hunter to produce fresh, approachable whites for the cafe market. This is one such: a delightful, early-drinking semillon from the Poole's Rock second label: gently herby with fresh lemongrass flavours, clean cut, fine and vibrant with good concentration, depth and length.

2008 D'Arenberg 'Dry Dam' Riesling $16.95

Like many of the D'Arenberg wines this overdelivers. I'm not usually a fan of McLaren Vale whites (except for Coriole's Fiano) but this is a very good wine at a terrific price. There are attractive florals, a touch of talc on the nose, impressive intensity and power, freshness, pristine flavours and a restrained floral finish.

2007 D'Arenberg 'Last Ditch' Viognier $19.95

Predominantly sourced from the Adelaide Hills and 100% barrel-fermented in old oak so there is structure without overt oakiness. I'm attracted by its gentle viscosity, clean, fresh, dried herb flavours, orange blossom and supple minerally finish.

2007 Domain Day 'One Serious' Riesling $19.95

Robin Day's Barossa Valley vineyard is at an elevation of 450 metres in the Barossa Ranges and adjoins the Eden Valley on two sides. Not surprisingly, it's admirably suited to riesling. This is classy and priced to please: there are floral and lavender fragrances, vibrant lemony, lime flavours and some persistent minerality to finish.

2007 Frankland Estate 'Isolation Ridge' Riesling $27

The flagship wine from this Frankland River producer is restrained and fine with perfumed talc, rich, concentrated lemon juice flavours and impressive weight, finishing lean and minerally. Immeasurably lifted by the right dish: say, pad thai with a squeeze or two of lime.

2008 Grosset Semillon Sauvignon Blanc $32

I know this is one of the most expensive wines in the book and it's an SBS blend. I know, I know. But I think it's Jeff Grosset's best-ever example of the style, and he's been making Australia's best – or one of its best – examples of the blend for 18 years, blending Clare Valley semillon with Adelaide Hills sauvignon. This is pristine, intense and cool with white peach and nectarine flavours, is tight and fine with taut, mouth-puckering racy acidity. It has the zestiness and tangy, slatey minerality that is a feature of the very best young whites.

2007 Hanging Rock 'Jim Jim' Sauvignon Blanc $27

I'm not sure if wine writers are supposed to have favourite wines but if I were to have some favourites, then this ultra-cool sauvignon would be one of them. I first tried this vintage before it had been released while tasting at the winery in the shadow of that iconic Hanging Rock. I loved its fragrance and noted that it would be terrific in time. I tasted it recently in a blind tasting and it showed just as I might have hoped it would: floral, appley, intense cool fruit flavours, yet the wine has some restraint, nicely balanced with a fine-knit finish that is zesty and long.

2008 Henschke 'Peggy's Hill' Riesling $20

I guess the Henschkes must despair of me. They now have three attractive rieslings under their label – 'Greens Hill', 'Louis' and 'Peggy's Hill' – and for a third year in a row I've liked their cheapest most of all. There's some talc and lemony fragrances, mid-palate juiciness and pure, fine and delicate yet intense, lemony flavours. It's still young, tight and coiled but promises heaps.

2007 Hesketh 'Hidden Garden' Sauvignon Blanc $20

Jonathon Hesketh is a negociant who buys parcels of fruit, has them made into wine, and markets them. For the past two years, he has made exemplary Marlborough sauvignon and markets it as 'Hidden Garden'. The 2007 has intense green bean character, zesty, ripe tropical flavours, a riot of lychee and gooseberry with gentle acidity to finish.

2007 Higher Plane 'South by Southwest'
Semillon Sauvignon Blanc $22

Higher Plane has been taken over by Juniper Estate but still sells wine under its second label 'South by Southwest'. It's situated well to the south of the Margaret River township and so makes some excellent cool whites. This is fresh and vibrant with tangy gooseberry and pineapple flavours, some succulence and zesty acidity that cleanses the palate.

2007 Houghton 'Pemberton' Chardonnay $29.50

Understated Houghton winemaker, Ross Pamment, has been responsible for making some superb chardonnay under this label and that of Brookland Valley for several years. There's some matchstick complexity on the nose while the wine is a model of restraint: very cool melony flavours with slatey minerally notes. There's great finesse, an attractive mouthfeel and some savouriness to finish.

2007 Keith Tulloch Semillon $26

Keith Tulloch is one of Australia's most articulate winemakers with one of our best cellar doors, a not-to-be-missed experience if you're in the Hunter Valley. Here's a very good example of what the region does best – fresh youthful semillon. This is very fine with intense lemon citrus, lanolin and cut grass flavours, wonderful zestiness before a clean, dry finish that invigorates.

2008 Kirrihill 'Single Vineyard' Riesling $18

Arguably the best Clare riesling you'll find for less than $20: a hint of talc, bold, rich, powerful lemony flavours and a fresh, tangy finish of some considerable length.

2007 Leeuwin Estate 'Sibling' Sauvignon Blanc Semillon $23.50

While there's plenty of flavour there, this is a textural rather than flavour-driven example of the style that Margaret River does so well. All of Leeuwin's semillon is barrel fermented without taking on any cedary characters. There's restraint, gentle persistent flavours with some green pea characters lifting the mid-palate before a crisp, dry finish.

2007 Mountadam 'Barossa' Chardonnay $18

Since Con Moshos left Petaluma to take over at Mountadam, this important Eden Valley winery has shown dramatic improvement. To be fair to its previous owners, I believe that the process of revitalising the Mountadam vineyards began under the stewardship of Moët & Chandon. I saw this chardonnay in a pretty bleak tasting of unwooded chardonnays and it shone like the proverbial beacon. Don't get this confused with the more expensive Mountadam Chardonnay but enjoy it for its bright, cool mandarin flavours, vibrance and intensely concentrated ripe sweet fruit.

2007 Mountadam Riesling $25

A quintessential Eden Valley riesling that is still fresh and vital, weighty and powerful with intense lemon and lime flavours, finishing with cleansing minerally acidity.

2007 Neagles Rock Riesling $19

Here's another sub-$20 Clare riesling, this time from the small, rapidly improving family winery of Steve Wiblin and Jane Willson: it's a powerful – even full-throttle – white with dense, concentrated lime juice flavours that linger.

2007 Nugan Estate Sauvignon Blanc $19.95

Just when you think you've got the guys at Nugan Estate taped, they surprise you. I know that they've been buying fruit from Coonawarra and McLaren Vale but this is the first time they've ventured over the Nullarbor – to pick up some Margaret River fruit to satisfy a shortfall with the 2007 vintage. I'm glad they did as this wine is packed full of flavour – lightly grassy, herbal, green bean characters – and finishes fine, clean and dry. Well priced, too.

2007 Peos 'Four Aces' Chardonnay $25

Manjimup, a small country town known locally for its vegetable growing and forestry, has had no national profile. The success of its truffle industry has changed that. Vic Peos has been working hard to redress the balance and his family vineyard has been impressing, especially with chardonnay and shiraz. This has full, ripe melony, peachy flavours of good intensity, is delicately balanced, and finishes crisp and fresh.

2007 Pipers Brook Pinot Gris $21.50

A wine like this helps you understand why Pipers Brook has been keen to highlight its potential with aromatics such as riesling, gewurztraminer and pinot gris. It has a delicious savoury quality, its viscosity gives it an attractive mouthfeel, while its ultra-dry finish allows the wine to linger in the memory.

2007 Poachers Ridge Riesling $18.95

Alex and Janet Taylor have established a vineyard plus a delightful cafe/cellar and deck with sweeping views at Poachers Ridge, not far from Mt Barker. It's one of a number of ventures making a visit to this sub-region of the Great Southern a much more pleasant and interesting experience. Here is an attractive floral riesling that has depth and concentration of stone-fruit flavours, good balance and a long, dry finish.

2007 Redgate Sauvignon Blanc Semillon $20

Winemaker Simon Keall has been working hard to lift quality at this Margaret River property, with pleasing results. This is the best Redgate white for some time: delicious passionfruit and tropical fruit flavours, a varietal tang from the sauvignon blanc, and a fresh, clean finish that zings.

2007 Robert Channon Verdelho $24.50

This Granite Belt winery has an enviable record with verdelho, consistently winning gold medals and trophies with the variety at local shows. While this vintage is not the best performed of the line, it is a delicious drink: sparklingly clean and vibrant with ripe tropical flavours, a hint of complexity on the mid-palate and a fresh, soft finish.

2006 Rockford Riesling $19

While Robert O'Callaghan and the team at Rockford are best known for their fabulous sparkling red and their superb 'Basket Press' Shiraz, they make reliably good whites and sell them at very attractive prices. This intense riesling is showing the benefit of a touch of bottle age with its powerful, full-on, gently toasty flavours, delicate balance and zesty, clean finish.

2007 Rosemount Estate 'Show Reserve' Sauvignon Blanc $20.95

I can't quite get my head around a well-established Aussie company releasing a Kiwi sauvignon under its 'Show Reserve' label. Still, it's a well-priced quality Marlborough white: clear varietal expression in the grassy spectrum, green bean even, with vibrant, zesty acidity to finish.

2006 Saracen Estates Chardonnay $30

Saracen Estates is situated in the northern part of the Margaret River region on the opposite side of Caves Road from the opulent Laurance. The locals are imagining a future battle of the cellar doors, as Saracen is working on its own stunning cellar door complex. Whatever the truth about the rivalry, the stakes have been lifted in this part of the region. Luke Saraceni does nothing by half and former Leeuwin winemaker Bob Cartwright consults to Saracen. This is a fascinating chardonnay: big, rich, fleshy with honey, even caramel, characters and sweet creamy texture, before it tightens on the mid-palate and finishes vibrant, intense, dry and persistent.

2007 Seppelt 'Jaluka' Chardonnay $26.95

Here's a classy Victorian chardonnay from Seppelt: fresh, clean and succulent with cool, white peach and nectarine flavours and a subtle, restrained finish.

2008 Shaw & Smith Sauvignon Blanc $25

While it looks incredibly youthful and unevolved, this classic Aussie sauvignon blanc shows all the intensity of cool, green-skinned fruit, delicious zestiness and refreshing tanginess that makes it a perennial favourite.

2007 Starvedog Lane Pinot Grigio $21

A fabulous, well-priced Adelaide Hills pinot grigio from a Constellation label: lively, plump and varietal with impressive savoury characters that are rich and concentrated, before a clean, dry finish.

2007 Trevelen Farm Riesling $20

John and Katie Sprigg are the first of the Great Southern producers that you come to as you head south along the Albany Highway. This is their stand-out wine from the home block at Cranbrook: fine, focused and delicately balanced, intense lemony flavours and a clean, zippy finish.

2006 Vasse Felix Chardonnay $25

Margaret River's first winery is currently among the region's best performers. This is one of the best-value chardonnays you'll find from the region. It has soft, fresh flavours, restrained cedary oak and attractive, ripe, sweet fruit before a lively, dryish finish.

2007 Vasse Felix Semillon $25

I've sometimes found the Vasse Felix Semillon a bit too oaky. No such problem here as the wine is all zesty green bean flavours, easy drinkability and fresh, cleansing acidity.

2005 Yarra Park Sauvignon Blanc $27.50

A newish vineyard in the Yarra, close to Mount Mary, owned by Stephen and Rosalind Atkinson with this wine made by Phil Kerney at Willow Creek – although Mac Forbes has since taken over the vinicultural reins. This is very much in the style of sauvignon developed by the Yarra winemakers which looks to complexity and mouthfeel rather than chasing varietal character. It may take some getting used to but I love it. The wine may need a vigorous swirl to clean up the nose but there's yeasty, leesy complexity, almost a hint of durian, impressive viscosity and a beguiling mouthfeel which goes on and on. It's a wine for contemplation rather than gulping.

Pink Wines over $15

2008 Charles Melton 'Rose of Virginia' $26.50

Here is a traditional Barossa family winery that seems to have no problem getting the kind of exposure its outstanding range of wines deserves. This grenache blend is consistently among Australia's best rosés: ripe, sweet, gently macerated cherry fruit, richly concentrated, powerful, a hint of sweetness and fresh, cleansing acidity.

2006 Farr Rising Saignee $20

Earlier this year, I enjoyed a major tasting of the wines of Farr Rising – made by Nick Farr, son of *Gourmet Traveller Wine*'s 2001 Winemaker of the Year, Gary. The chardonnays and pinot noirs were very fine to exceptional. I also loved the Farr Rising Saignee, especially from 2004 and 2006. This is a rosé made from pinot noir that in 2006 has strawberries and cream flavours, silky texture and a restrained ultra-dry finish. Very impressive.

2007 Geoff Merrill Grenache Rosé $18.50

Here is a long-time favourite of *Quaff*'s, risen slightly in price but showing all the characters that we've admired over the years: ripe, sweet redcurrant and strawberry flavours, some sweetness in the mid-palate and on the finish but all brought into line by crisp, refreshing acidity.

2007 Jacobs Creek 'Reserve' Shiraz Rosé $15.95

It's easy to see why this second release of the newest wine in the range is so popular that 300,000 cases were made: ripe, vibrant, sweet raspberry and redcurrant flavours yet with a finish that is crisp, clean and dry. Delicious.

2008 Turkey Flat Rosé $23

Another of Australia's most dependable rosés from an unlikely yet regular blend of grenache, shiraz, cabernet sauvignon and dolcetto. It was a very good 2008 vintage for Barossa rosés and this is soft, round and deliciously easy to drink, aromatic with bright red berry fragrances, long, deep flavours before a slight grip gives the finish a dry feel.

Red Wines over $15

2005 Abbey Creek Pinot Noir $24

> Mike and Mary Dilworth have a tiny Porongurup vineyard which produces sublime riesling and this delicious pinot noir, made by the talented Rob Diletti at nearby Castle Rock. It has wonderfully fragrant spicy aromas, sweet, ripe redcurrant and raspberry flavours of good intensity and silky smooth texture. Varietal and classy.

2006 All Saints Shiraz $22.50

> This is one of the pleasant drinking reds that I've seen from the Browns and their Rutherglen winery. It has richness and concentration of flavour, is smooth with almost silky texture, and soft, fine tannins: easy drinking and succulent.

2005 Angelicus Pinot Noir $22

> John and Sue Ward are establishing a new Pemberton vineyard, not far from Smithbrook, and are producing some attractive wines. This is a very good up-front pinot with excellent varietal character – intense red cherries, dark plums – neat balance and silky smooth texture.

2006 Battle of Bosworth Cabernet Sauvignon $24

> The Bosworths have been growing grapes in McLaren Vale since the 1840s, with Joch progressively converting the mature vineyard to organic viticulture since 1995, and it is now producing some excellent reds. Here, vanilla bean and dark plum flavours slide down the throat all too easily: there's concentration, power, weight too.

2006 Battle of Bosworth Shiraz $24

This organically grown shiraz is becoming one of the stars of the region. There's a portion of cane-cut, Amarone-style fruit added to give complexity and a ripe pruney note. Lavish brambly blackberry pastille flavours, silky smooth texture, good depth and richness in balance with substantial tannins.

2007 Black Chook Shiraz Viognier $18

Ben Riggs can sure pack some concentrated fruit into his reds. This has ripe blackberry and dark plum flavours, plenty of vanillin oak and substantial though approachable tannins. It's big, robust and full flavoured with velvety texture: not elegant but sure to find an appreciative audience.

2006 Blue Pyrenees Merlot $18

I saw this as part of the *Quaff* tastings and it topped the field. The winery obviously believes that it will be on special for less than $15. My advice, of course, is that if you see it at that price, snap it up. It's dense, powerful and rich with concentrated blackcurrant and chocolate flavours, neatly integrated fruit, oak and tannins, and so is nicely approachable. This book exists to find wines like this. Quaff on!

2005 Brown Brothers Tempranillo $16.90

The Spanish variety tempranillo loves the warmth of Heathcote and Brown Brothers has plenty of the variety planted there. If you don't know the grape, here's a good wine to introduce you. This is dense and powerful, quite weighty, savoury rather than sweet, earthy redcurrant – almost beetroot – and with substantial tannins. It does need a hearty, slow-cooked lamb shank or oxtail dish to complement it.

2006 Brown Hill 'Chaffers' Shiraz $18

This is a small Margaret River winery, situated at Rosa Glen to the south of the township. Its wines are well priced and not for the faint of heart. This shiraz has plenty of smoky oak, deep peppery flavour, generous, velvety texture and powerful, fine tannins.

2005 Chalice Bridge 'Calamus' Shiraz Merlot Cabernet Sauvignon $16.95

This is a rare example of a good-to-very-good Other Red Blend. Chalice Bridge has a large vineyard at Rosa Glen to the south of Margaret River in an area that I would generally expect to be better for whites than reds. The wine is soft, round and textural with good depth and juicy dark berry flavours. There's some firmness to finish and yet the wine is approachable. Try with bangers and mash plus a rich gravy.

2004 Chalk Hill Shiraz $21

I tasted a wider selection of the Chalk Hill range this year and was impressed by what I saw of this McLaren Vale vineyard. My bottle of the shiraz needed decanting or a vigorous swirl after it was opened but once that was done, I was captivated by the wine's soft, velvety texture, fleshy red berry flavours and smooth tannin structure. Enjoy the McLaren Vale approachability.

2006 Charles Cimicky 'Trumps' Shiraz $19

As a result of being distributed by Angoves, the traditional Barossa family company of Charles Cimicky is beginning to get the kind of national exposure it deserves. This is a well-priced fruit bomb that has deep blackberry and vanilla flavours, smooth, velvety texture and heaps of oak and tannin.

2005 D'Arenberg 'Cadenzia' Grenache Shiraz Mourvedre $25

The McLaren Vale's liveliest winery has never performed better and it's been buying up old vineyards in the McLaren Vale at an amazing rate, at a time when everyone else is playing the quiet, cautious game. Its access to substantial volumes of quality, old-vine grenache is clearly shown in wines like this. There are raspberry and redcurrant jelly flavours, a pleasing juiciness in the mid-palate and a finish that is long and fine.

2006 D'Arenberg 'High Trellis' Cabernet Sauvignon $19.95

There's value in this McLaren Vale cabernet: rich, ripe and deep blackcurrant and dark plum characters, silky smooth in the mid-palate and substantial, approachable tannins.

2006 D'Arenberg 'Laughing Magpie' Shiraz Viognier $29.95

Serve this at a dinner party and most of your friends will think you've spent a whole lot more. It's amazingly floral (unless you realise that it has a whopping 10% viognier added), very soft, round and fleshy, with a lifted quality in the mid-palate, dark plums and red cherry flavours flow through the mid-palate and linger on a gentle, long finish. Seductive.

2007 De Bortoli 'Gulf Station' Pinot Noir $20.95

This is a Yarra Valley pinot from Steve Webber, Sarah Fagan and the team at De Bortoli and represents fantastic value. It's fragrant, silky smooth, even fleshy, with admirable varietal character – some wild dark cherry and mulberry characters with gamey notes – finesse, and long lingering flavours.

2005 Dukes Cabernet Sauvignon $22

A small vineyard in the Porongurups that is home to Hilde and Duke Ransom. While the wines are not widely available, there'll always be a warm welcome at the cellar door. This cabernet shows some elegance: spicy cinnamon nutmeg aromas, reasonably rich and concentrated dark plum flavours, some fleshiness and firm, grippy tannins that beg for a robust beef stew.

2007 Ferngrove Shiraz $18.95

Here's terrific value from Kim Horton and the team at the best performer of the Frankland River wineries: deep, dense vanilla bean and dark berry flavours, velvety texture and heaps of oak make it a robust style. There's plenty of extraction and tannin but the weight to match. Not elegant but full of flavour.

2007 Flying Fish Cabernet Merlot $22

Although most of its income comes from contract winemaking, Flying Fish has its own vineyards and a successful label of its own, which sources fruit only from Margaret River. It often offers excellent value for money, as it does here. Clever winemaking gives this wine attractive, red succulence and approachability while preserving vibrant, deep and rich blackcurrant and dark plum flavours, fleshy texture and restrained, drying tannins.

2007 Flying Fish 'Italian Job' $22

There are precious few of the Italian varieties planted in Margaret River and so this is not only a rare but a surprisingly approachable blend of sangiovese and nebbiolo. The grapes are sourced from a grower who has both the varieties just a few kilometres from Flying Fish. It's intense, rich, uncomplicated yet easy to like.

2005 Fraser Gallop Cabernet Sauvignon $25

Situated close to Bussell Highway at the opposite end of Metricup Road from Moss Wood and Evans & Tate, Fraser Gallop is a spare-no-expenses new establishment with experienced and talented winemaker Clive Otto calling the shots. This cabernet represents an auspicious debut: dried herbs and spicy oak aromas, dense blackcurrant flavours and fine, drying tannins.

2005 Goundrey 'G' Shiraz Viognier $21

As I write, the team at Houghton is reeling from the news that many of the vineyards that they have nurtured throughout the state and the winery at Goundrey will be sold. While there won't be much disappointment at the loss of the winery, the viticultural team has done some brilliant work on the Goundrey vineyards. This is a terrific example of what they have achieved: a well-priced, cool-climate shiraz that, at last, fulfils the promise that Goundrey has shown for so long. Its juicy – even succulent – rich, ripe and concentrated dark plummy fruits are neatly integrated with classy oak. Approachable.

2006 Hewitson 'Miss Harry' Shiraz Grenache Mourvedre $22

Dean Hewitson makes the kind of red that I love to drink. Here's a good example: an excellent, approachable example of old-vine Barossa shiraz, grenache and mourvedre blended so that its richness of vibrant blackberries, velvety texture and pleasing approachability combine to seduce the lucky consumer.

2006 Hugh Hamilton 'Rascal' Shiraz $24.95

This is one of the best reds I've seen from the black sheep of the family's McLaren Vale operation. While it needs a good swirl before sniffing, it will appeal to those who love rich, concentrated reds with lavish oak and full-throttle power.

2005 Juniper Crossing Cabernet Merlot $17.95

The vineyard at Juniper Estate was planted in 1973, although the current ownership dates back only to 1999. The vineyards have been rejuvenated and the winery, under the direction of its experienced and well-performed winemaker, Mark Messenger, has impressed. This wine is from Juniper's regional range and you'll be hard pressed to find better value in Margaret River than this elegant, well-structured cabernet from an excellent vintage: velvety, packed with rich, concentrated blackcurrant and dark plum flavours and neatly balanced.

2006 Kalleske 'Clarry's' Grenache Shiraz $19

Troy and Tony Kalleske are part of the Artisans of the Barossa, a group of small producers dedicated to preserving the rich traditions of the region. While many of their wines are sourced from dry-grown old vines and are consequently priced beyond everyday drinking, this easy-drinking Barossa grenache blend represents outstanding value. It has bright, primary red berry fruit and lush texture with a gentle, gravelly edge.

2006 Lucas Estate Cabernet Merlot $35

I did a large tasting of Queensland wines while I was up there for the annual Tourism Conference and found there were plenty of wines to love. Two of the top half-dozen were from Lucas Estate (this and the 2005 'Partners' Merlot Cabernet) and were made by husband-and-wife team Colin Sellers and Louise Samuel. Sadly Colin has passed on – but Louise will continue the tradition they established together. If you're in the Granite Belt, call in. This has impeccably pure fruit with rich, ripe, sweet blackcurrant flavours, fleshy texture and supple, fine-knit tannins. A wine of impressive finesse.

2006 Margan Shiraz $20

Away from the hustle and bustle of Hunter Central, the Margan family winery is nestled among some of the region's most picturesque scenery at Broke. There's an excellent cafe with an adventurous wine list, too. This is brilliantly priced: vibrant, fleshy and packed with bright, dark berry fruit and a hint of restrained oak, held together with an attractive, supple tannin structure. Succulent and approachable.

2005 Nugan Estate 'Parish' Shiraz $23.95

Most of the wines from the Riverina's Nugan Estate are sourced from the family's King Valley vineyards. It also takes cabernet from Coonawarra and shiraz from McLaren Vale. This is from Matthew Nugan's own McLaren Vale vineyard: there's plenty of spicy oak, ripe, deep flavours and silky smooth texture.

2006 Paul Conti 'The Tuarts' Tempranillo $17.50

The Conti family winery was established at Wanneroo on the outskirts of Perth in 1958, with Paul's son Jason now doing the hard work. This wine is sourced from two vineyards in the warm Swan District and is medium-bodied with some intense, juicy redcurrant flavours which make for attractive drinking.

2005 Peter Lehmann Cabernet Merlot $19.50

I tasted this with the *Quaff* cab merlots where it shone. I think it's well priced at full tote odds: if you can get it cheaper it would be a bargain. This is crammed with ripe, concentrated dark plum and red cherry flavours, has some pleasing juiciness, smooth texture and soft, fine tannins. The kind of wine that made the Peter Lehmann reputation.

2005 Peter Lehmann Shiraz $19.50

These make a great pair. My heart would pick the Shiraz every time but tasted blind there was nothing between it and the Cabernet Merlot in quality terms. There's a wonderful softness about this: juicy redcurrant, blackberry and dark chocolate flavours with a hint of spice. There's plenty of oak but it's nicely integrated and the tannins are ripe and in balance. All in all, it's a great quaffer from an excellent vintage.

2005 Picardy Shiraz $20

While I haven't always been a fan of the Picardy Shiraz (preferring the elegance of its Pinot), in 2005 the Pannells have nailed it so comprehensively that I'm thinking of eating humble pie. This is superb: supple, round and fleshily smooth with good depth and density of blackberry and mulberry flavours, a cedary oak edge, and substantial ripe, fine-knit tannins that are held in check by its fruit weight. Power and opulence make this a bargain of monumental proportions. Limited availability. Quaff on!

2006 Picarus Cabernet Sauvignon $20

Picarus is a new label sourcing its fruit from Wrattonbully on the Limestone Coast. There's a richness and concentration of ripe blackcurrant flavour and velvety texture that give this appeal.

2005 Poachers Ridge 'Louis' Merlot $23.95

This was chosen by James Halliday to represent Australia in the annual Tri-Nations competition between Australia, New Zealand and South Africa last year. It won the merlot trophy: spicy, concentrated dark berry flavours, silky smooth, almost lush, with a firm finish.

2005 Seppelt Victorian Shiraz $18.95

Over the past few years, there have been some attractive, well-priced wines under the Seppelt Victorian label. This has substantial American oak and supple tannins yet has the depth of dark berry fruit to balance that. It's a robust, full-throttle red with rich, concentrated flavours and fleshy texture that will ensure widespread appeal.

2006 Shingleback Cabernet Sauvignon $24.95

John and Kate Davey picked up the Jimmy Watson Trophy with their previous vintage D Block Cabernet, so this wine has excellent pedigree. It's a terrific, approachable McLaren Vale cabernet that is aromatic, has ripe, concentrated blackcurrant flavours, richness and power – lushly fruity.

2004 Smithbrook Merlot $24

This Pemberton vineyard was purchased in 1998 by Brian Croser for Petaluma and is still part of the group. The vineyard obviously makes a significant contribution to the Lion Nathan brands as they've added a winery to the property. The Smithbrook label, however, appears to remain in the grip of a carefully planned subliminal marketing campaign. With the 2004 Merlot there are earthy, gamey, savoury characters to balance its ripe dark berry flavours and nutmeggy, oaky characters. There are heaps of tannins and extract but, with food, it's a complex, fascinating drink.

2006 St Hallett 'Faith' Shiraz $21

That Stuart Blackwell and his team do spring the occasional surprise (actually, not too occasionally). This time I was wondering where the ultra-concentration of blackberries had come from. I was bowled over by the dense, opulent, briary fruit, velvety texture and fleshy approachability of this wine. I would have expected a much more expensive Barossa shiraz. A benchmark for shiraz under $30.

2006 Tar & Roses Shiraz $17.95

Don Lewis and Narelle King source the fruit from Heathcote – and it shows in this full-bodied, powerful shiraz that is ultra-concentrated, deeply flavoured yet approachable.

2006 Tar & Roses Tempranillo $25

If you enjoy a good oak whack, there's a lot to like about this juicy, fleshy and succulent tempranillo. It's crammed with raspberry and blackcurrant flavours, has smooth texture and substantial tannins held in check by the fruit weight.

2005 Tatachilla Shiraz $22

Tatachilla is another fragment of the Lion Nathan portfolio, with winemaker Fanchon Ferrandi in charge of producing wine for the McLaren Vale label. Here is a well-priced shiraz that has it all: fragrance, succulence and fleshy texture with ripe blackberry flavours and gently firm approachability.

2006 Taylors 'Eighty Acres' Cabernet Shiraz Merlot $16.95

The Clare Valley's largest producer has another newish label. This will appeal to those who love powerful, oaky reds that have plenty of richness, vanilla bean and dark berry flavours, and smooth texture. Still a touch raw but that will disappear with time.

2005 Trevelen Farm 'Reserve' Merlot $23

In 2005, John Sprigg sourced a parcel of Frankland River fruit that has made a pleasantly drinkable (if oaky) red: supple and round with red berry and vanilla flavours.

2006 Western Range 'Julimar' Shiraz Viognier $24.50

> Western Range, one of two largish wineries in the Perth Hills region, has its winery in the Chittering Valley but sources fruit from throughout the region. It has a superb 2006 Chardonnay and this delicious red. While some may be put off by the labelling, this is one of the great Western Australian bargains: juicy, densely concentrated with oak and extract matched by fruit weight, luscious blackberries and vibrant vanilla.

2005 Wills Domain Shiraz $23

> From Margaret River's northern reaches comes a vineyard better known for its whites but showing form here with an attractive shiraz – redcurrant and blackberry pastille, smooth and ripe.

2006 Wordsworth Cabernet Merlot $24

> Here is the best wine yet from this newish Harvey producer with an impressive cellar door: concentrated blackcurrant, redcurrant and dried herb flavours, succulent, smooth and approachable. Perfect with the local beef.

2006 Wynns Cabernet Shiraz Merlot $18.95

> A return to form for an old favourite, showing the benefit of the viticultural improvements Fosters has made in Coonawarra. The 2006 Wynns red blend is soft, round and fleshy, with restrained power, good depth of red berry flavours and balanced tannins. Pleasantly approachable.

2007 Wynns Shiraz $20.95

> This is part of the Wynns revolution. The 2007 vintage wasn't a great one in Coonawarra and there was none of the Wynns flagship 'Michael' Shiraz. Still, this is fabulous at the price: soft, ripe, supple and fleshy with lively redcurrant and blackberry flavours and succulent fine tannins. Excellent drinking.

Stickies over $15

These are arguably Australia's three best stickies.

2006 Cookoothama Botrytis Semillon (375 ml) $22.95

A series of outstanding vintages has placed the Cookoothama among the country's finest examples of what noble rot can do to a wine. It's gently fragrant with hints of marmalade and honey, intense honeyed apricot, orange rind flavours that are full and sweet on the mid-palate, very fine and elegant, beautifully balanced, smoothly viscous before zesty acidity provides a pristine, dry finish of considerable finesse.

2006 De Bortoli 'Noble One' Botrytis Semillon (375 ml) $33.95

Since 1982, this has been regarded as Australia's best dessert wine and the inspiration behind the Riverina's push to feature botrytis semillon as the finest achievement of the region. This is dense, powerful, opulent and complex: some cedary notes are still there on the nose while the palate highlights concentrated apricot, lemon rind and marmalade flavours, satiny smooth texture and fine, penetrating acidity that freshens the finish and leaves it dry and satisfying.

2008 Mount Horrocks 'Cordon Cut' Riesling (375 ml) $35

Clare Valley riesling never looks more seductive than in this superbly consistent stickie. In spite of the tricky 2008 vintage, this is a classy wine, light of body but intense in flavour: gently fragrant with deep honey flavours, some lemon and lime notes, lush, sweet texture, finishing dry and long.

Fortifieds over $15

Campbells Rutherglen Tokay $18.30

This is a superb example of entry-level Rutherglen tokay and shows why this region is famous for its world-class fortifieds. There's a lightness of touch about the wine, while it has richly concentrated sweet toffee, butterscotch and honey flavours with a hint of tea leaf, lush texture before a refreshingly dry finish. An excellent everyday tokay from one of the region's great wine families.

De Bortoli 8 Year Old Tawny $22.95

As well as being crammed with honey, toffee, caramel, chocolate and dried fruit flavours, this has a softness and an easy-drinking quality that makes it a sure bet on a winter's night – and plenty of other occasions too.

Grant Burge 10 Year Old Tawny $27.50

Barossa shiraz has become so popular that we tend to forget how important fortified wines have been in the region's history – and how good they can be. This is a complex, powerfully concentrated tawny with satiny smooth texture, rich toffee malt and earthy, mushroomy flavours before a finish that neatly balances brandy spirit and fruit weight.

Imported Wines over $20

WHITES

2007 Casa Silva 'Reserva' Sauvignon Gris $24

I wondered, at first, if this was a blend of sauvignon blanc and pinot gris, but it's a different (new to me) grape variety from Casa Silva in Chile's Colchagua Valley. I enjoyed its slightly honeyed floral aromas, delicately viscous texture and attractively dry finish.

2006 Henry Pelle Menetou-Salon $24.95

This is a very different style of sauvignon blanc than those found in Marlborough and around Australia – and it's well worth trying. This is from one of the Loire Valley's less well-known appellations, Menetou-Salon (so it's cheaper than if it came from somewhere like Sancerre). It is vibrant, fresh and spotless with restrained minerally characters that are clearly savoury rather than fruity, before thrilling, racy acidity cleanses the palate. Exclusive to Vintage Cellars.

2006 Lawsons 'Dry Hills' Gewurztraminer $22.95

The New Zealand Grapegrowers decided to run some seminars in Australia to show us that they could do more than sauvignon blanc and pinot noir. This was one of the wines they chose. Wow! It stopped me in my tracks with its hedonistic, dramatically aromatic, viscous, almost lush texture, fine honeysuckle, rose petal and lychee flavours and delicate, dry finish. That's cool climate for you.

2007 Stoneleigh Pinot Gris $20.95

I've tasted this a couple of times, once in my regular tastings and once when the New Zealand Grapegrowers ran a seminar in Perth to show us that the country could do more than sauvignon blanc and pinot noir. This was one of the wines they chose to show how well New Zealand could do the aromatics. It's the most impressive Kiwi pinot gris I've seen, with such ethereal aromas, such depth of varietal character – spicy, pear flavours, almost musk-like – terrific satiny smooth viscosity and a long, dry finish. Imported by Pernod Ricard.

REDS

2006 Casa Silva 'Gran Reserva' Cabernet Sauvignon $24

I did a major tasting of Chilean wines that are being imported into this country and was impressed by many of the offerings. This drinks well, being pleasantly approachable and rich, ripe and plummy with smooth texture and substantial though fine-knit tannins.

2006 Casa Silva 'Gran Reserva' Carmenère $24

The Bordeaux variety does particularly well as a stand-alone variety in Chile and it's very easy to love: fleshy, velvety texture, rich, full, wild dark berry flavours with pleasing minerality to finish.

How to track down the bargains

HOW TO TRACK DOWN THE BARGAINS

If you're keen on finding bargains in bottle-shop land, one of the best things you can do is make a nuisance of yourself – in the nicest possible way, of course. Make sure the people behind the counter at your favourite wine retailer know you're interested in drinking good wine, and are looking out for bargains. If they're doing their job properly, they should nurture you as a valued customer – your buying cheap wine on a regular basis is just as important as one-off sales of stratospherically priced icon wines to people who'll never come back.

As a wine consumer, you have two choices. You can either sit back and let the wine shops seduce you into buying this week's unbeatable special through their advertising and their promotions and their smooth talking. Or you can make a little bit of effort and discover your own specials all by yourself. Here are a few tips to help you become a well-informed, quick-thinking, quick-quaffing wine bargain explorer.

Some Tips for the Bargain Hunter

Read about wine

Yeah, I know the old saying, 'Don't believe everything you read', but in the cause of finding good value, I reckon you should take notice of at least some of the many thousands of words published about wine in newspapers and magazines and over the internet each week.

One way to keep *Quaff 2009* up to date throughout the next year is to become a subscriber to the *Quaff* website. It's free. All you need to do to subscribe to *Quaff*'s Wines of the Week is to go to **www.quaff.com.au** then click on 'Subscribe' and give us your email address. You'll receive a weekly email telling you what the Wines of the Week are.

Buy up big

In the short term, buying wines by the case, or dozen bottles, can be a real pain in the back pocket. But I thoroughly recommend it, as you are almost guaranteed to receive a discount. If you can't afford it yourself, get together with a group of mates and each chip in the cost of a couple of bottles – that way you spread the cost but share the benefits. Maybe it's a sign of the times but many retailers will also offer a better price to customers who buy half a dozen bottles at a time.

Where the bloody hell are you?

No amount of reading beats experience. Most Australians live a few hours' drive from a wine region. There's no excuse not to get into the car and visit a couple of cellar doors. Australia's winemakers want to know where you are and, if you're not out and about visiting them, why not?

At the cellar doors, you'll (hopefully) get an idea of how to taste wine for maximum enjoyment, and you'll be able to (hopefully) learn about how grapes are grown. Cellar doors are also great places to find discounted wines – bargain bins, ends of vintage, reduced to clear, often on tasting before you buy. Many wineries have mailing lists that you can join, and offer exclusive bargains to mailing list members. If

you can't visit a cellar door, then many wine shops have in-store tastings, and wine exhibitions are enjoying increasing popularity.

Spend more money

You probably don't expect to be told this in a book dedicated to
finding the most enjoyment for the least expense, but a big tip is to
try and spend a little bit more on wine than you did last time (within
reason, of course, and without plunging yourself into debt ...
although I can talk). If you're used to spending $8, try a $10.95 bottle
of the same variety or style next time you visit the bottle shop; if $12
is your usual spend, lash out on a $15 bottle – and so on. Another idea
is to buy these slightly more expensive bottles once a week for a
special Friday or Saturday dinner or a long Sunday lunch with
friends. You may very well think that the extra money isn't worth it –
in which case, revert to the old favourites and save yourself some
cash. But you may also find that the slightly pricier wines can offer
better value for money – in other words, by increasing your spend by
20%, you can increase your enjoyment by 100%. You won't know,
though, unless you try for yourself.

Don't believe the hype

Be very careful out there. Australian wine marketing departments are
incredibly clever at attaching little shiny round stickers to their labels
that look uncannily like medals won at some wine show or other.
Don't be fooled. Read the shiny stickers carefully. If they tell you the
wine has won two bronze medals, it means it was judged to be fair to
average quality on two separate occasions. If they tell you the winery
was judged Winery of the Year at some international drinks fair in
Finland in 1986, be cautious. And even if they tell you that the wine in
the bottle has won a string of gold medals and trophies, while you can
be safe that the wine is well made, that's no guarantee you will like it.
Again – and again and again – try before you buy, if you can.

Finding the Wines

This index will enable you to source further information on any of the wines reviewed in *Quaff*, such as your nearest local stockist. The name by which the wine is known (the winery or label) is followed by the name of the distributor (where appropriate), a website or email address and a contact number.

ABBEY CREEK
abbeycreek@iprimus.com.au   (08) 9853 1044

ACROBAT
www.yourwinecompany.com   (08) 8338 3200

ADINFERN
www.adinfern.com   (08) 9755 5272

ALKOOMI
www.alkoomiwines.com.au   (08) 9855 2229

ALL SAINTS
www.allsaintswine.com.au   (02) 6035 2222

ALTOS LAS HORMIGAS (GRAPE EXPECTATIONS)
sally@grapeexp.com.au   (08) 9212 9100

AMBERLEY (CONSTELLATION WINES)
www.cwines.com.au   1800 088 711

ANGAS BRUT (YALUMBA)
www.yalumba.com   (08) 8112 4200

ANGOVES
www.angoves.com.au   (08) 8580 3100

ANNIES LANE (FOSTERS)
www.fostersgroup.com   1300 651 650

ARADON (VINTAGE CELLARS)
www.vintagecellars.com.au   1300 366 084

ARROGANT FROG (DAN MURPHY'S)
www.danmurphys.com.au   1300 723 388

BANROCK STATION (CONSTELLATION WINES)
www.cwines.com.au   1800 088 711

BARKING OWL (MILLBROOK)
www.millbrookwinery.com.au   (08) 9525 5796

BATTLE OF BOSWORTH
www.battleofbosworth.com.au   (08) 8556 2441

BAY OF FIRES (CONSTELLATION WINES)
www.cwines.com.au   1800 088 711

BEELGARA
www.beelgaraestate.com.au   (02) 6966 0223

BERRI (CONSTELLATION WINES)
www.cwines.com.au   1800 088 711

BLACK CHOOK (PENNY'S HILL)
www.pennyshill.com.au   (08) 8556 4460

BLEASDALE
www.bleasdale.com.au   (08) 8537 3001

BLUE PYRENEES
www.bluepyrenees.com.au   (03) 5465 3203

BODEGA NORTON (VINTAGE CELLARS)
www.vintagecellars.com.au   1300 366 084

BROWN BROTHERS
www.brown-brothers.com.au   (03) 5720 5500

BROWN HILL
www.brownhillestate.com.au   (08) 9757 4003

BULLER
www.buller.com.au   (03) 5037 6305

BURGANS (VINTAGE CELLARS)
www.vintagecellars.com.au   1300 366 084

CALABRIA (WESTEND)
www.westendestate.com   (02) 6964 1506

CALDER GROVE
www.newtarwines.com.au   (03) 5024 5704

CAMPBELLS
www.campbellswine.com.au   (02) 6032 9458

CAPEL VALE
www.capelvale.com   (08) 9727 0105

CAPE MENTELLE
www.capementelle.com.au   (08) 9757 0809

CARRINGTON (PERNOD RICARD)
www.pernod-ricard-pacific.com   1300 363 153

CARTWHEEL (FOSTERS)
www.fostersgroup.com   1300 651 650

CASA SANTOS (VINTAGE CELLARS)
www.vintagecellars.com.au   1300 366 084

CASA SILVA (GRAPE EXPECTATIONS)
ally@grapeexp.com.au   (08) 9212 9100

CASELLA
www.casellawines.com.au   (02) 9330 4721

CELESTIAL BAY
www.celestialbay.com.au   (08) 9450 4191

CHALICE BRIDGE
www.chalicebridge.com.au   (08) 9433 5200

CHALK HILL
www.chalkhill.com.au   (08) 8556 2121

CHAPEL HILL
www.chapelhillwine.com.au   (08) 8323 8429

CHARLES CIMICKY (ANGOVES)
www.angoves.com.au   (08) 8580 3100

CHARLES MELTON
www.charlesmeltonwines.com.au   (08) 8563 3606

COCKATOO RIDGE (FINE WINE PARTNERS)
www.finewinepartners.com   1300 668 512

COCKFIGHTERS GHOST (POOLES ROCK)
www.poolesrock.com.au   (02) 9563 2500

COLDSTONE (VICTORIAN ALPS WINERY)
www.victorianalpswinery.com   (03) 5751 1992

CONCHA Y TORO (VINTAGE CELLARS)
www.vintagecellars.com.au   1300 366 084

CONO SUR (VINTAGE CELLARS)
www.vintagecellars.com.au   1300 366 084

COOKOOTHAMA (NUGAN ESTATE)
www.nuganestate.com.au   (02) 6962 1822

COOLABAH (PERNOD RICARD)
www.pernod-ricard-pacific.com   1300 363 153

CORTE GIARA (NEGOCIANTS)
www.negociantsaustralia.com   (08) 8112 4210

CRITTENDEN
www.crittendenwines.com.au   (03) 5981 8322

CUTTLEFISH (FLYING FISH COVE)
www.flyingfishcove.com   (08) 9755 6600

D'ARENBERG
www.darenberg.com.au   1800 882 335

DASHWOOD (VINTAGE CELLARS)
www.vintagecellars.com.au   1300 366 084

DE BORTOLI
www.debortoli.com.au   (02) 9636 6033

DEAKIN ESTATE
www.deakinestate.com.au   (03) 5029 1666

DOMAIN DAY
www.domainday.com.au   (08) 8524 6224

DUKES
www.dukesvineyard.com   (08) 9853 1107

DUNES (YALUMBA)
www.yalumba.com   (08) 8112 4200

EDWARDS
www.edwardsvineyard.com.au   (08) 9755 5999

ELDERTON
www.eldertonwines.com.au   (08) 8568 7801

FARR RISING
www.byfarr.com.au   (03) 5281 1979

FERNGROVE
www.ferngrove.com.au   (08) 9227 0297

FIFTH LEG (FOSTERS)
www.fostersgroup.com   1300 651 650

FISHBONE (BLACKWOOD)
www.fishbonewines.com   (08) 9756 0088

FLYING FISH COVE
www.flyingfishcove.com   (08) 9755 6600

FOOLS BAY (HENTLEY FARM)
www.hentleyfarm.com.au   (08) 8562 8427

FOUR SISTERS (TAHBILK)
www.tahbilk.com.au   (03) 5794 2555

FOX CREEK
www.foxcreekwines.com   (08) 8556 2403

FRANKLAND ESTATE
www.franklandestate.com.au   (08) 9855 1544

FRASER GALLOP
www.fgewines.com.au   (08)9755 7553

GEOFF MERRILL
www.geoffmerrillwines.com   (08) 8381 6877

GIESEN (NEGOCIANTS)
www.negociantsaustralia.com   (08) 8112 4210

GNANGARA (MCWILLIAMS)
www.mcwilliams.com.au   1800 800 584

GOUNDREY (CONSTELLATION WINES)
www.cwines.com.au   1800 088 711

GRANT BURGE
www.grantburgewines.com.au   (08) 8563 7522

GROSSET
www.grosset.com.au   (08) 8849 2175

GROWERS
www.thegrowers.com   (08) 9755 2121

HAMELIN BAY
www.hbwines.com.au   (08) 9389 6020

HANGING ROCK
www.hangingrock.com.au   (03) 5427 0542

HARDYS (CONSTELLATION WINES)
www.cwines.com.au   1800 088 711

HENKELL (MCWILLIAMS)
www.mcwilliams.com.au   1800 800 584

HENSCHKE
www.henschke.com.au   (08) 8564 8223

HESKETH
www.heskethwinecompany.com.au   0419 003 144

HEWITSON
www.hewitson.com.au   (08) 8443 6466

HIGH COUNTRY (MIRANDA WINES)
www.australianvintage.com.au   (02) 8345 6377

HIGHER PLANE
www.higherplanewines.com.au   (08) 9451 7277

HOUGHTON (CONSTELLATION WINES)
www.cwines.com.au   1800 088 711

HUGH HAMILTON
www.hughhamiltonwines.com.au   (08) 8323 8689

INNOCENT BYSTANDER (FINE WINE PARTNERS)
www.finewinepartners.com   1300 668 512

JACOBS CREEK (PERNOD RICARD)
www.pernod-ricard-pacific.com   1300 363 153

JEAN PIERRE (DE BORTOLI)
www.debortoli.com.au   (02) 9636 6033

JIM BARRY
jbwines@jimbarry.com   (08) 8842 2261

JUNIPER
www.juniperestate.com.au   (08) 9451 7277

KALLESKE
www.kalleske.com   0412 136 964

KEITH TULLOCH
www.keithtullochwine.com.au   (02) 4998 7500

KINGSTON ESTATE
www.kingstonestatewines.com   (08) 8130 4500

KIRRIHILL
www.kirrihillwines.com.au   (08) 8842 1233

KONO (VINTAGE CELLARS)
www.vintagecellars.com.au   1300 366 084

LAMONTS
www.lamonts.com.au   (08) 9296 4485

LAWSONS DRY HILLS (WINESTOCK FINE WINE)
www.winestock.com.au   (03) 9418 7899

LEAPING LIZARD (FERNGROVE)
www.ferngrove.com.au   (08) 9227 0297

LEASINGHAM (CONSTELLATION WINES)
www.cwines.com.au   1800 088 711

LEEUWIN ESTATE
www.leeuwinestate.com.au   (08) 9430 4099

LINDEMANS (FOSTERS)
www.fostersgroup.com   1300 651 650

LITTLE PENGUIN (FOSTERS)
www.fostersgroup.com   1300 651 650

LOGAN
www.loganwines.com.au   (02) 6373 1333

LONG FLAT WINE CO (CHEVIOT BRIDGE)
www.cheviotbridge.com.au   (03) 9820 9080

LUCAS ESTATE
www.lucasestate.com.au   (07) 4683 6365

M CHAPOUTIER (FINE WINE WHOLESALERS)
www.fww.com.au   (08) 9314 7133

MARGAN
www.margan.com.au   (02) 6579 1317

MAXWELL
www.maxwellwines.com.au   (08) 8323 8200

MCGUIGAN (AUSTRALIAN VINTAGE)
www.australianvintage.com.au   (02) 8345 6377

MCPHERSON
www.mcphersonwines.com   (03) 9832 1700

MCWILLIAMS
www.mcwilliams.com.au   1800 800 584

MILES FROM NOWHERE (GRAPE EXPECTATIONS)
sally@grapeexp.com.au   (08) 9212 9100

MONTANA (PERNOD RICARD)
www.pernod-ricard-pacific.com   1300 363 153

MOONDAH BROOK (CONSTELLATION WINES)
www.cwines.com.au   1800 088 711

MORRIS (PERNOD RICARD)
www.pernod-ricard-pacific.com   1300 363 153

MOUNT HORROCKS
www.mounthorrocks.com   (08) 8849 2243

MOUNTADAM
www.mountadam.com.au   (08) 8564 1900

MT HURTLE (VINTAGE CELLARS)
www.vintagecellars.com.au   1300 366 084

NEAGLES ROCK
www.neaglesrock.com   (08) 8843 4020

NEPENTHE
www.nepenthe.com.au   (08) 8398 8888

NUGAN
www.nuganestate.com.au   (02) 6962 1822

OBIKWA (VINTAGE CELLARS)
www.vintagecellars.com.au   1300 366 084

O FOURNIER (GRAPE EXPECTATIONS)
sally@grapeexp.com.au   (08) 9212 9100

OISLY & THESEE (VINTAGE CELLARS)
www.vintagecellars.com.au   1300 366 084

OMBRA (VINTAGE CELLARS)
www.vintagecellars.com.au   1300 366 084

OMNI (CONSTELLATION WINES) www.cwines.com.au	1800 088 711
ORLANDO (PERNOD RICARD) www.pernod-ricard-pacific.com	1300 363 153
OXFORD LANDING (YALUMBA) www.yalumba.com	(08) 8112 4200
PAUL CONTI www.paulcontiwines.com.au	(08) 9409 9160
PEEL ESTATE www.peelwine.com.au	(08) 9524 1221
PENFOLDS (FOSTERS) www.fostersgroup.com	1300 651 650
PEOS www.peosestate.com.au	(08) 9772 1378
PETER LEHMANN www.peterlehmannwines.com.au	(08) 8843 4370
PFEIFFER www.pfeifferwines.com.au	(02) 6033 2805
PICARDY www.picardy.com.au	(08) 9776 0036
PICARUS www.winetrustestates.com	(02) 9949 9250
PIKES www.pikeswines.com.au	(08) 8843 4370
PIPERS BROOK (KREGLINGER) www.kreglingerwineestates.com	(03) 6382 7527
PITCHFORK (HAY SHED HILL) www.hayshedhill.com.au	(08) 9755 6046
PLANTAGENET www.plantagenetwines.com	(08) 9851 3111
POACHERS RIDGE www.prv.com.au	(08) 9857 6077
POET'S CORNER (PERNOD RICARD) www.pernod-ricard-pacific.com	1300 363 153
PORTONE (VINTAGE CELLARS) www.vintagecellars.com.au	1300 366 084
PRIMO ESTATE www.primoestate.com.au	(08) 8380 9442

QUEEN ADELAIDE (FOSTERS)
www.fostersgroup.com   1300 651 650

REDBANK (NEGOCIANTS)
www.negociantsaustralia.com   (08) 8112 4210

REDGATE
www.redgatewines.com.au   (08) 9757 6488

RENMANO (CONSTELLATION WINES)
www.cwines.com.au   1800 088 711

REX WATSON (THE WINE LIST)
www.wwgwines.com   (08) 8338 3200

RICHARD HAMILTON (LECONFIELD)
www.leconfieldcoonawarra.com.au   (08) 8323 8830

ROBERT CHANNON
www.robertchannonwines.com   (07) 4683 3260

ROCKFORD
www.rockfordwines.com.au   (08) 8563 2720

ROCK PAPER SCISSORS (VINTAGE CELLARS)
www.vintagecellars.com.au   1300 366 084

ROSEMOUNT ESTATE (FOSTERS)
www.fostersgroup.com   1300 651 650

SALTRAM (FOSTERS)
www.fostersgroup.com   1300 651 650

SANDALFORD
www.sandalford.com   (08) 9374 9374

SARACEN
www.saracenestates.com.au   (08) 9322 6642

SCARPANTONI
www.scarpontoni-wines.com.au   (08) 8383 0186

SEGURA VIUDAS (VINTAGE CELLARS)
www.vintagecellars.com.au   1300 366 084

SEPPELT (FOSTERS)
www.fostersgroup.com   1300 651 650

SEVENHILL
www.sevenhillcellars.com.au   (08) 8843 4222

SHAW & SMITH
www.shawandsmith.com   (08) 8398 0500

SHENTON RIDGE
www.shentonridge.com.au   (08) 9726 1284

SHINGLEBACK
www.shingleback.com.au   (08) 8370 2299

SIR JAMES (CONSTELLATION WINES)
www.cwines.com.au   1800 088 711

SMITHBROOK
www.smithbrook.com.au   (08) 9772 3557

STARVEDOG LANE (CONSTELLATION WINES)
www.cwines.com.au   1800 088 711

ST HALLETT
www.sthallett.com.au   1300 780 795

STONELEIGH (PERNOD RICARD)
www.pernod-ricard-pacific.com   1300 363 153

STONES (ANGOVES)
www.angoves.com.au   (08) 8580 3100

SUNSTONE (MCWILLIAMS)
www.mcwilliams.com.au   1800 800 584

SWINGS & ROUNDABOUT
www.swings.com.au   (08) 9756 6735

TAHBILK
www.tahbilk.com.au   (03) 5794 2555

TALINGA PARK (NUGAN ESTATE)
www.nuganestate.com.au   (02) 6962 1822

TALTARNI
www.taltarni.com.au   (03) 5459 7923

TAMINICK
www.taminickcellars.com.au   (03) 5766 2282

TAR & ROSES
lewis@eck.net.au

TATACHILLA (FINE WINE PARTNERS)
www.finewinepartners.com   1300 668 512

TAYLORS
www.taylorswines.com.au   (08) 8849 2008

T'GALLANT (FOSTERS)
www.fostersgroup.com   1800 007 282

THORN CLARKE
www.thornclarkewines.com

TOBACCO ROAD (VICTORIAN ALPS)
www.victorianalpswinery.com   (03) 5751 1992

TRENTHAM ESTATE
www.trenthamestate.com.au   (03) 5024 8888

TREVELEN FARM
www.trevelenfarmwines.com.au   (08) 9826 1052

TULLOCH (ANGOVES)
www.angoves.com.au   (08) 8580 3100

TURKEY FLAT
www.turkeyflat.com.au   (08) 8563 2851

TWO CHURCHES (VINTAGE CELLARS)
www.vintagecellars.com.au   1300 366 084

TYRRELLS
www.tyrrells.com.au   (02) 9889 4450

UPPER REACH
www.upperreach.com.au   (08) 9296 0078

VASSE FELIX
www.vassefelix.com.au   (08) 9756 5014

VICTORIAN ALPS
www.victorianalpswinery.com   (03) 5751 1992

VINTAGE CELLARS
www.vintagecellars.com.au   1300 366 084

WATER WHEEL
www.waterwheelwine.com   (03) 5437 3060

WESTEND
www.westendestate.com   (02) 6964 1506

WESTERN RANGE
www.westernrangewines.com.au   (08) 9571 8800

WILLESPIE
www.willespie.com.au   (08) 9755 6248

WILLOW BRIDGE
www.willowbridge.com.au   (08) 9728 0055

WILLS DOMAIN
www.willsdomain.com.au   (08) 9755 2172

WIRRA WIRRA
www.wirrawirra.com   (08) 8112 4210

WOLF BLASS (FOSTERS)
www.fostersgroup.com   1300 651 650

WOOP WOOP (PENNYS HILL)
www.pennyshill.com.au   (08) 8556 4460

WORDSWORTH
www.wordsworthwines.com.au   (08) 9733 4576

WYNDHAM ESTATE (PERNOD RICARD)
www.pernod-ricard-pacific.com   1300 363 153

WYNNS (FOSTERS)
www.fostersgroup.com   1300 651 650

XABREGAS
www.xabregas.com.au   (08) 9321 2366

XANADU
www.xanaduwines.com   (08) 9757 2581

YALUMBA
www.yalumba.com   (08) 8112 4200

YARRA PARK
www.yarrapark.com.au   (03) 9739 1960

YELLOWGLEN (FOSTERS)
www.fostersgroup.com   1300 651 650

YELLOW TAIL (CASELLA)
www.casellawines.com.au   (02) 6961 3000

YERING STATION
www.yering.com.au   (03) 9730 0156

ZILZIE
www.zilziewines.com   (03) 9417 1966

ZONTE'S FOOTSTEP
www.zontesfootstep.com.au   (08) 8537 3334

Recommended Retailers

Again, making friends with a good bottle shop is the best way to gain direct access to the great bargains – the one-offs and specials as well as the wines from small producers that haven't yet become cult buys (and are therefore unobtainable). This list has been put together by combining our own experience of various bottle shops around the country, and asking a network of contacts, including wine producers, wholesalers and distributors, where the best places to buy wine are located.

NATIONAL

Because of their size (between them they control about 40% of the market, and this percentage is growing), the Coles and Woolworths stores often have the best prices, but they can lack range and depth of wines on offer.

Coles – Vintage Cellars, 1st Choice, Liquorland

For store locations: 1300 366 084
www.vintagecellars.com.au
www.1stchoice.com.au
www.liquorland.com.au

Woolworths – Woolworths Liquor Stores, Dan Murphy's, BWS

For store locations:
www.beerwinespirits.com.au
www.danmurphys.com.au
www.woolworths.com.au/Storelocator

A group of wine merchants was formed to counter the power of the supermarket chains by working collaboratively while remaining independent.

The Alliance of Fine Wine Merchants

For store locations:
www.thewinealliance.com

A group of independent stores which use the marketing strength of the group to compete with the supermarket chains.

Cellarbrations

For store locations: www.cellarbrations.com.au

NEW SOUTH WALES

SYDNEY

Amato's Liquor Mart
267–277 Norton Street, Leichhardt, NSW 2040
(02) 9560 7628
amatos@amatos.com.au

Annandale Cellars
119 Johnston Street, Annandale, NSW 2038
(02) 9660 1947
sales@annandalecellars.com.au

Avalon Fine Wine and Foods
35 Avalon Parade, Avalon, NSW 2107
(02) 9918 3207
www.avalonfinewine.com.au

Best Cellars
91 Crown Street, East Sydney, NSW 2010
(02) 9361 3733
www.bestcellars.com.au

Camperdown Cellars
140 Parramatta Road, Camperdown, NSW 2050
(02) 9517 2000

City Cellars
54 Lime Street, Sydney, NSW 2000
(02) 9299 3385
www.citycellars.com.au

Five Ways Cellars
4 Heeley Street, Paddington, NSW 2021
(02) 9360 4242
iancook@fivewaycellars.com.au

Jim's Cellars
65 Edgeworth David Avenue, Waitara, NSW 2077
(02) 9489 7177
www.jimscellars.com

Jim's Cellars at Crows Nest

95 Willoughby Road, Crows Nest, NSW 2065
(02) 9437 6688
www.jimscellars.com

Kemenys

137–147 Bondi Road, Bondi, NSW 2026
(02) 8383 5280 or 13 88 81
www.kemenys.com.au

Liquor Brothers

3A Anella Avenue, Castle Hill, NSW 2154
(02) 9680 7311
www.liquorbrothers.com.au

Newport Bottler

386 Barrenjoey Road, Newport, NSW 2106
(02) 9997 6721

North Sydney Cellars

MLC Building, Shop 4, 105 Miller Street, North Sydney, NSW 2060
(02) 9954 0090
www.northsydneycellars.com.au
shop@northsydneycellars.com

Palm Beach Wine Co.

1109 Barrenjoey Road, Palm Beach, NSW 2108
(02) 9974 4304
www.palmbeachwineco.com

Polifroni Cellars

Shop 1, 169 Annangrove Road, Annangrove, NSW 2156
(02) 9679 0144

Porters Liquor

For store locations: www.portersliquor.com.au
customerservice@portersliquor.com.au
(02) 9816 3044 or toll free 1800 688 226

Ultimo Wine Centre

21/99 Jones Street, Ultimo, NSW 2007
(02) 9211 2380
www.ultimowinecentre.com.au

Wine Culture
23 Babbage Road, Roseville Chase, NSW 2069
(02) 9882 1788
www.wineculture.com.au

OUTSIDE SYDNEY

Elanora Hotel
41 Victoria Street, Gosford East, NSW 2250
(02) 4325 2026
www.elanorahotel.com.au

Lambton Fridge
86 Elder Street, Lambton, NSW 2299
(02) 4957 1274

Leura Cellars
169–171 Leura Mall, Leura, NSW 2780
(02) 4784 1122

Oxford Tavern
47 Crown Street, Wollongong, NSW 2500
(02) 4228 3892

Toowoon Bay Cellars
153–155 Bay Road, Toowoon Bay, NSW 2261
(02) 4332 7459

Tosti Cellars
136 Wentworth Street, Port Kembla, NSW 2505
(02) 4274 1315
www.tosticellars.com.au

VICTORIA

MELBOURNE

6J's Wine Merchants

Shop 814, Prahran Market,
163 Commercial Road, South Yarra, VIC 3141
(03) 9824 2751
www.6js.com.au

Armadale Cellars

813–817 High Street, Armadale, VIC 3143
(03) 9509 3055
www.armadalecellars.com.au

City Wine Shop

159–161 Spring Street, Melbourne, VIC 3000
(03) 9654 6657
www.citywineshop.net.au

Cloudwine Cellars

317 Clarendon Street, South Melbourne, VIC 3205
(03) 9699 6700
766 Burke Road, Camberwell, VIC 3124
(03) 9882 0954
www.cloudwine.com.au

Europa Cellars

Shop G3, 150 Wellington Parade, East Melbourne, VIC 3002
(03) 9417 7220

International Fine Wines

19–21 Russell Street, Abbotsford, VIC 3067
(03) 8415 0206
www.ifw.com.au
orders@ifw.com.au

King & Godfree

293 Lygon Street, Carlton, VIC 3053
(03) 9347 1619
www.king&godfree.com.au
kgodfree@aol.com

McCoppins

165 Johnston Street, Fitzroy, VIC 3065
(03) 9417 5089
mccoppins-fitzroy@iinet.net.au

Parkhill Cellars

43–45 Errol Street, North Melbourne, VIC 3051
(03) 9328 1132
www.parkhillcellars.com

Prince Wine Store

177 Bank Street, South Melbourne, VIC 3205
(03) 9686 3033
2A Acland Street, St Kilda, VIC 3182
(03) 9536 1155
www.princewinestore.com

Randall's

186 Bridport Street, Albert Park, VIC 3206
(03) 9686 4122
www.randalls.net.au

Rathdowne Cellars

348 Rathdowne Street, Carlton North, VIC 3054
(03) 9349 3366
www.rathdownecellars.com.au

Winebins

58 Commercial Road, Prahran, VIC 3181
(03) 9510 5424

OUTSIDE MELBOURNE

Corky's Liquor

2–8 Breed Street, Traralgon, VIC 3844
(03) 5174 1211
www.corkys.com.au
admin@corkys.com.au

Jack's Wine and Spirits

901 Sturt Street, Ballarat, VIC 3350
(03) 5332 1176
www.jackswine.com.au

KM Lynch
116 Fairy Street, Warrnambool, VIC 3280
(03) 5562 4939

Murray Esplanade Cellars
2 Lesley Street, Echuca, VIC 3564
(03) 5482 6058
mecellars@ozemail.com.au

Neuschafers
90 Mercer Street, Geelong, VIC 3220
(03) 5229 8871

Randall the Wine Merchant
324 Pakington Street, Newtown, VIC 3351
(03) 5223 1141
www.randalls.net.au
newtown@randalls.net.au

SOUTH AUSTRALIA

ADELAIDE

East End Cellars
22–26 Vardon Avenue, Adelaide, SA 5000
(08) 8232 5300
www.eastendcellars.com.au
wine@eastendcellars.com.au

Edinburgh Cellars
7 High Street, Mitcham, SA 5062
(08) 8373 2753
www.edinburgh.com.au
cellars@edinburgh.com.au

Fassina Liquor Merchants
37–39 Oaklands Road, Somerton Park, SA 5044
(08) 8295 7707
admin@fassina.com.au

Goodwood Cellars

125 Goodwood Road, Goodwood, SA 5034
(08) 8271 7481
goodwoodcellars@toucangroup.com.au
www.goodwoodcellars.com

Melbourne Street Cellars

93 Melbourne Street, North Adelaide, SA 5006
(08) 8267 1533
ms93@tpg.com.au

Norwood Hotel

97 The Parade, Norwood, SA 5067
(08) 8431 1822

Parade Cellars

Shop 15, 161–175 The Parade, Norwood, SA 5067
(08) 8332 0317
paradecellars@optusnet.com.au

Royal Oak Hotel

123 O'Connell Street, North Adelaide, SA 5006
(08) 8267 2488

Wine Underground

121 Pirie Street, Adelaide, SA 5000
(08) 8232 1222
www.wineunderground.com.au

OUTSIDE ADELAIDE

Berri Resort Hotel

Riverview Drive, Berri, SA 5342
(08) 8582 1411 or 1800 088 226
www.berriresorthotel.com
ontheriver@berriresorthotel.com

Fidler & Webb

64 Commercial Street East, Mount Gambier, SA 5290
(08) 8725 3038
fidwebb@datafast.net.au

Grand Tasman Hotel

94 Tasman Terrace, Port Lincoln, SA 5606

(08) 8682 2133

www.grandhotel.com.au

gthotel@internide.on.net

QUEENSLAND

BRISBANE

1st Choice Liquor Superstore

577 Settlement Road, Keperra, QLD 4054

(07) 3351 0499

201 Ferry Road, Southport, QLD 4215

(07) 5556 5155

www.1stchoice.com.au

Jindalee Hotel

Sinnamon Road (cnr Goggs Road), Jindalee, QLD 4074

(07) 3710 5858

john.norris@coles.com.au

Cru Bar & Cellar

22 James Street, Fortitude Valley, QLD 4006

(07) 3252 1744

www.crubar.com

The Gap Tavern

21 Glenquarie Place, The Gap, QLD 4061

(07) 3366 6090

www.gaptavern.com.au

The Grape Group

446 Lutwyche Road, Lutwyche, QLD 4030

(07) 3257 0404

www.thegrape.com.au

Paddington Tavern

186 Given Terrace, Paddington, QLD 4064

(07) 3369 0044

www.maguireshotels.com.au

Stewarts Wine Co

Racecourse Road (cnr Dobson Street), Ascot, QLD 4007
1300 138 838 or (07) 3216 4944
www.stewartswineco.com.au

Story Bridge Hotel

200 Main Street, Kangaroo Point, QLD 4169
(07) 3391 2266
www.storybridgehotel.com.au
info@storybridgehotel.com.au

The Wine Emporium

Shop 47, 1000 Ann Street, Fortitude Valley, QLD 4006
(07) 3252 1117
www.thewineemporium.com.au
thevalley@thewineemporium.com.au

Wine@era

102 Melbourne Street, South Brisbane, QLD 4101
(07) 3255 2033
www.erabistro.com.au

OUTSIDE BRISBANE

Austral Hotel

189 Victoria Street, Mackay, QLD 4740
(07) 4951 3288
www.australhotel.com.au

Barrier Reef Hotel

33 Wharf Street, Cairns, QLD 4870
(07) 4051 4245

Courthouse Hotel

51 Nerang Street, Southport, QLD 4215
(07) 5532 0122

Seaview Hotel

56 The Strand, North Ward, QLD 4810
(07) 4771 5005
www.seaviewhotel.com.au
seaview@pubzco.com.au

Smithfield Tavern

Captain Cook Highway, Smithfield, QLD 4878

(07) 4038 1411

Villa Noosa Hotel

Mary Street, Noosaville, QLD 4566

(07) 5430 5555

www.villanoosa.com.au

WESTERN AUSTRALIA

PERTH

Barossa Cellars

278 Railway Parade, Leederville, WA 6007

(08) 9381 1770

Bicton Cellars

221 Preston Road, Bicton, WA 6157

(08) 9339 1917

www.bictoncellars.com.au

Chateau Guildford

124 Swan Street, Guildford, WA 6055

(08) 9377 3311

Dan Murphy's Westminster

22 Culloton Crescent, Balga, WA 6061

(08) 9342 2568 or 1300 723 388

www.danmurphys.com.au

Grants of Cottesloe

24 Railway Street, Cottesloe, WA 6011

(08) 9384 3920

grantsofcottesloe@iinet.net.au

Harborne & Cambridge Cellars

252 Cambridge Street, Wembley, WA 6014

(08) 9388 3033

Invinity Fine Wine Brokers
Level 1, 58 Kishorn Road, Mount Pleasant, WA 6153
(08) 9315 3777
www.invinity.com.au
info@invinity.com.au

Lamont Wine Store
12 Station Street, Cottesloe, WA 6011
(08) 9385 0666
www.lamontswinestore.com.au

La Vigna
302 Walcott Street, Mount Lawley, WA 6050
(08) 9271 1179
www.lavigna.com.au
lavigna@lavigna.com.au

Liquor Barons Herdsman
Shop 5, 1 Flynn Street, Churchlands, WA 6018
(08) 9387 4222
herdsman@liquorbarons.com.au

Liquor Barons Mount Lawley
654 Beaufort Street, Mount Lawley, WA 6050
(08) 9271 0886
mtlawley@liquorbarons.com.au

Liquor Barons South Perth
23 Mends Street, South Perth, WA 6050
(08) 9367 1001
southperth@liquorbarons.com.au

Old Bridge Cellars
221 Queen Victoria Street, North Fremantle, WA 6159
(08) 9335 2702
oldbridge@iinet.net.au

Paddington Ale House
141 Scarborough Beach Road, Mount Hawthorn, WA 6016
(08) 9242 3077
www.paddo.com.au
info@paddo.com.au

Re Store

231 Oxford Street, Leederville, WA 6007
(08) 9444 9644
72 Lake Street, Northbridge, WA 6003
(08) 9328 1877
admin@the-re-store.com.au

Rossmoyne Cellars

5 Third Avenue, Rossmoyne, WA 6148
(08) 9457 6439

Scarborough Cellars

166 Scarborough Beach Road, Scarborough, WA 6019
(08) 9341 1437
scarcell@bigpond.com

Sexton Cellars

30 Sexton Road, Inglewood, WA 6052
(08) 9370 4111
ingewinestore@yahoo.com.au

Swanbourne Cellars

103 Claremont Crescent, Swanbourne, WA 6010
(08) 9384 2111
swanycellars@bigpond.com
admin@swanbournecellars.com

OUTSIDE PERTH

Dan Murphy's Albany

9 York Street, Albany, WA 6330
1301 723 388
www.danmurphys.com.au

ACT

1st Choice Liquor Superstore

170 Melrose Drive, Phillip, ACT 2606
(02) 6122 8901
www.1stchoice.com.au

Braddon Cellars
11 Lonsdale Street, Braddon, ACT 2612
(02) 6247 2440

Campbell's Liquor Discount
4 Blamey Place, Campbell, ACT 2612
(02) 6247 1366

George's Liquor Stable
17 Dundas Court, Phillip, ACT 2606
(02) 6285 3075

Jim Murphy's Market Wine Cellars
19 Mildura Street, Fyshwick, ACT 2609
(02) 6295 0060
jcellars@bigpond.net.au

Local Liquor
Wattle Place, Lyneham, ACT 2602
(02) 6249 7263
www.localliquor.com.au

The Wine Shed
Shop 27, Belconnen Markets, Lathlain Street, Belconnen, ACT 2617
(02) 6251 3781
wineshed@grapevine.com.au

TASMANIA

HOBART

Aberfeldy BWS
124 Davey Street, Hobart, TAS 7000
(03) 6211 6633
www.beerwinespirit.com.au

Gasworks 9/11 Bottleshop
Shop 3, 2 Macquarie Street, Hobart, TAS 7000
(03) 6214 7525
bwiggers@vantagegroup.com.au

OUTSIDE HOBART

Alexander Hotel
79 Formby Road, Devonport, TAS 7310
(03) 6424 2671
sbraddey@goodstone.com.au

Club Hotel
22 Mount Street, Burnie, TAS 7320
(03) 6432 3668

Gunners Arms Tavern
23 Lawrence Street, Launceston, TAS 7250
(03) 6331 3891

Pinot Shop
135 Paterson Street, Launceston, TAS 7250
(03) 6331 3977
www.pinotshop.com

TRC Hotel
131 Paterson Street, Launceston, TAS 7250
(03) 6331 3424
trc@bigpond.com

NORTHERN TERRITORY

Beachfront Hotel
342 Casuarina Drive, Rapid Creek, NT 0810
(08) 8985 3000
beachfront@hotkey.net.au

Hidden Valley Tavern
Stuart Highway, Berrimah, NT 0828
(08) 8984 3999
info@hiddenvalleytavern.com.au

Northside Foodland
3 Hearn Place, Alice Springs, NT 0870
(08) 8952 2754

Parap Fine Foods

40 Parap Road, Parap, NT 0820
(08) 8981 8597
www.parapfinefoods.com
sales@parapfinefoods.com

Parap Village Tavern

15 Parap Road, Parap, NT 0820
(08) 8981 2191
parapvillagetavern@bigpond.com

Vintage Cellars

27 Cavenagh Street, Darwin, NT 0800
(08) 8941 7345
www.vintagecellars.com.au

Wine Clubs and Online Retailers

There are disadvantages to joining a direct-selling wine club like Cellarmasters or The Wine Society – the main ones being the inability to try before you buy, and the fact that you have to take the rough with the smooth: not every wine you are sent will be a masterpiece of the vintner's art (that's one way that costs are kept so low). The same applies to buying wine over the internet.

WINE CLUBS

Cellarmasters
1800 500 260
www.cellarmasters.com.au

Liquorland Direct
1300 300 640
www.liquorlanddirect.com.au

Vintage Cellars
1300 366 084
www.vintagecellars.com.au

Wine Selectors
1300 303 307
www.wineselectors.com.au

The Wine Society
1300 723 723
www.winesociety.com.au

ONLINE STORES

The following websites often have some excellent prices, and all have a good range, including some smaller-producer, harder-to-get wines and, in many cases, a wide range of cleanskins.

Judging by their newspaper advertising and the strong recommendations of my pal, Jon Cook, the biggest of these may well be:

www.getwinesdirect.com

www.auscellardoor.com.au
www.auswine.com.au
www.boccaccio.com.au
www.boutiquewineries.com.au
www.ckdirect.com.au
www.cleanskins.com
www.discountwines.com
www.nicks.com.au
www.organicwine.com.au
www.ozliquormart.com.au
www.prospectwines.com.au
www.tastingroom.com.au
www.winelarder.com.au
www.winepool.com.au
www.winestar.com.au
www.winezy.com.au

SEARCH ENGINES

The Wine Searcher website is very powerful and extremely useful in finding wines – and their wildly varying prices – all around the world, not just in Australia. If you buy a lot of wine online, it's worth signing up to the Pro version:

www.wine-searcher.com

And despite its limited scope, the Wine Robot search engine can return some great bargains:

www.winerobot.com.au

Decoding the jargon

A quick wine glossary

A QUICK WINE GLOSSARY

MAX ALLEN

aromatic

A catch-all phrase that refers to wines with strong positive aromas, such as the powerfully varietal smells of good sauvignon blanc.

austere

A wine that tastes a little mean, hard and tight, as though the flavours are there, but the wine doesn't want to give them to you.

bottle-aged

If wines are left alone in the bottle for a number of years, they can develop complex, savoury bottle-aged characters, quite distinct from the fresh, fruity characters they had when they were young.

buttery

Some winemaking techniques – for example, malolactic fermentation and lees contact – can contribute a rich, creamy, buttery aroma and flavour to wooded whites such as chardonnay.

chalky

Steely, flinty, minerally. The words used to describe really dry white wines.

chewy

Chewy red wines have lots of grape-skin extracts in them, giving a strong impression of being really thick and full in the mouth.

clean

Simply, a wine that is free of faults: fresh-tasting, pleasant. 'Clean' can occasionally be a more loaded description, implying that the wine is technically correct, but not overly exciting.

closed

Or dumb. A wine that tastes like a shadow of its former self. The opposite, of course, is 'open' or 'forward': a wine that seems to be wearing all its flavours on its sleeve and showing off a bit.

coarse

Wine that's a bit unsubtle and rough-tasting is 'coarse' – a bit too dry, a bit too sharp. 'Unbalanced' might be more correct; 'rustic' might be more diplomatic.

complex

You take a sniff and smell blackberries. You take another sniff and smell cherries. Another and wet undergrowth. Another and just a hint of fresh cracked pepper. This is a complex wine.

dusty

The tannins in young red wines can give a bizarre impression of being dry and dusty along the sides and back of your tongue.

elegant

A word you see a lot on wine labels. It means exactly what it says: the wine is balanced, tastes fine, is pleasing – all without knocking your tastebuds around.

fat

A wine that fills every corner of your mouth and sits plumply, but perhaps a little clumsily, on your tongue.

faults

Things can go wrong with wine at any stage, from when the grapes are picked to when the bottle is opened. The symptoms and causes of the most common faults are listed following. If you find them in your wine, you have every right to complain, send back the bottle to the waiter, or ask for an exchange from the bottle shop.

fault 1: hazy appearance

In wines that should be crystal clear – like young riesling, for example – cloudiness can indicate bacterial spoilage.

fault 2: dull, brown colour

The wine has come into contact with too much oxygen due to a leaky cork, has oxidised and is on its way to becoming vinegar. This is more relevant for white wine.

fault 3: musty, mouldy smells

Occasionally caused by the wine being stored in dirty, old barrels, but most often a musty smell is caused by cork taint. Cork is prone to all kinds of contamination which can, in turn, taint the wine, making it taste 'corked' – flat, dull, even quite rank – like mouldy cardboard.

fault 4: smells like rotten eggs or burnt matches

Rotten eggs is hydrogen sulphide, which can form in a wine during fermentation. It is usually easily dealt with by the winemaker, but occasionally creeps into the bottle. Burnt match smells are due to excessive sulphur dioxide, which is a preservative added to most wines.

fault 5: vinegary or solvent smells

These come from excessive levels of volatile acids (known as VA), and/or ethyl acetate. The volatile acids (such as the vinegar acid, acetic acid) are the ones we can smell. Ethyl acetate is formed when acetic acid combines with alcohol. A little VA can add complexity and lift the aromas of a wine; a lot can make it smell like nail-polish remover.

'fault' 6: tiny, crunchy crystals in the bottle

You can come across these in sweet white wines and older red wines. They are *not a fault*, but natural tartrate crystals that can develop when the wine ages or gets too cold. They do not affect the wine's taste or quality.

finish

The aftertaste. As in: 'This full-bodied shiraz has an extraordinarily long finish that lingers in the mouth for a minute.' As with so much else in life, the longer the better, obviously.

firm

Solid, taut, tense, sturdy – a more pleasant version of 'austere'.

fleshy

A more positive way of saying 'fat': a wine with plenty of palpable fruit in the mouth.

floral

Literally smelling like flowers.

full-bodied

A wine that fills the mouth and seems to impose on the palate – in contrast with medium- and light-bodied wines, which make a less imposing impression.

green or herbaceous

There are two main reasons why a wine might smell grassy, herbaceous or green. It's either meant to – like sauvignon blanc – or the grapes that made it were under-ripe – like some red wines grown in very cool climates.

hot

Wine made from over-ripe grapes grown in warm climates can produce a hot-tasting burn of alcohol at the back of the throat. The fruit in those wines can also taste a bit jammy.

lifted

Sometimes the delicate, spicy or fragrant aromas in a wine seem to be lifted towards your nose by some invisible hand.

long

A very good thing. A wine that has a long finish is one whose flavours seem to go on and on and on for seconds, right down the back of your throat.

nose

How the wine smells. As in: 'This young chardonnay has a marvellous nose of apples, vanilla and oatmeal.' If you're feeling posh, you could use the word 'bouquet'.

nutty

Sometimes wines can taste nutty because of the barrels they're stored in (chardonnay, for example), and sometimes it's a flavour found in the grape variety they're made from (pinot gris).

oaky or woody

Again, a catch-all term that covers all sorts of descriptions from the vanilla-like smell of new oak barrels used to age the wine before bottling to the cedarwood smell of old cabernet, and also covering the toasty smells, the spicy smells, the dusty smells and even the dirty old barrel smells.

rich

Wine with lots of viscosity, flesh, substance and fruit.

smoky

Some white grapes such as gewürztraminer and pinot gris can make wines with a dusky, smoky perfume; and sometimes barrels can give wine that's stored in them a different, more pungent, smoky or charred aroma.

spicy

Like smoky aromas, spicy characters can come from the grape varieties – the pepperiness of shiraz, for example – or the barrel – the clove and aniseed aromas of some (French) oak.

stalky

A little stalkiness (in wines that have been fermented with a few of the grape stems included) can be a good, complex thing. A lot just makes the wine taste green and stalky.

tannic

Tannins are the astringent bit of grape skins. Grapes with thick skins and lots of tannin like cabernet can produce 'tannic' wine, which tastes particularly dry and savoury, like the liquid is gripping onto your tongue and gums before you swallow.

thin

The opposite of fat, and hardly ever a good thing. Thin wines, wines that are really neutral-tasting, that seem hollow and lean, are usually the result of overcropped grapes and poor winemaking.

varietal

Literally, 'tastes like the grape variety the wine was made from'.

zingy

Crisp, fresh, lively, juicy, tangy, zesty, lemony, citrusy – these are all good words for wines with noticeable but pleasant acidity. 'Sharp' and 'sour' are used when the acid's unbalanced and unpleasant.

Index of
wines

Now you can **Quaff** online!

The Quaffing experience doesn't have
to end when you put this book down.

To receive weekly reviews of great-value
wines throughout the year,
subscribe for free at

www.quaff.com.au

and hear from us each Friday with our
Wine of the Week.

We'll keep you informed throughout
the year as the best wines
under $15 hit the market.

Don't forget to tell your friends,

and **Quaff** on!